Codependent No More

WORKBOOK

Codependent No More

WORKBOOK

Melody Beattie

HAZELDEN®

OTHER BOOKS BY MELODY BEATTIE

Beyond Codependency

Choices

Codependent No More

Codependents' Guide to the Twelve Steps

52 Weeks of Conscious Contact

Finding Your Way Home

Gratitude

The Grief Club

Journey to the Heart

The Language of Letting Go

The Language of Letting Go Journal

The Lessons of Love

More Language of Letting Go

Playing It by Heart

Stop Being Mean to Yourself

Hazelden
Center City, Minnesota 55012
hazelden.org

Library of Congress Cataloging-in-Publication Data

Beattie, Melody.
  Codependent no more workbook / Melody Beattie.
    p. cm.
  Companion volume to Melody Beattie's Codependent no more: how to stop controlling others and start caring for yourself.
  Includes bibliographical references.
  ISBN 978-1-59285-470-7
  1. Codependency—Problems, exercises, etc. 2. Substance abuse—Patients—Rehabilitation—Problems, exercises, etc. I. Beattie, Melody. Codependent no more. II. Title.
  RC569.5.C63B433 2011
  616.86'9—dc22
                        2010043011

Author's Note:
As an independent contractor and freelance writer, I relied on professional research, personal experience, conclusions, and opinions to form this workbook. Although I've used expert opinions as resources, this book doesn't necessarily reflect any viewpoint or opinions except my own. Neither the book nor I am affiliated with, represent, or work for any organization or treatment program. Names and certain details have been changed to ensure privacy and anonymity, but all stories in here are true; none are fictionalized or composites. Even anonymous quotes came from real people.

Editor's Note:
This publication is not intended as a substitute for the advice of health care professionals. Alcoholics Anonymous, AA, and the Big Book are registered trademarks of Alcoholics Anonymous World Services, Inc.

                13   3 4 5 6

Cover design by Nick Caruso
Interior design and typesetting by Madeline Berglund

For the straightforward, delightful (anonymous) Mrs. Bee, who knew what this workbook needed to be and cared enough to tell me; and old-timers, newbies to codependency recovery, and everyone in between who wants to continually evolve because they know healing is experiential, is experimental, and "more shall be revealed."

CONTENTS

ACKNOWLEDGMENTS

THANK YOU TO RENAISSANCE MALIBU AND SAL PETRUCCI

FOR THEIR GREAT QUOTES AND COOPERATION

AND TO SAGE KNIGHT,

WHOSE EDITING HELP LIKELY KEPT ME ALIVE.

INTRODUCTION:

Suggested Uses for This Workbook

This book will benefit those attending family group meetings for a loved one in addiction treatment, and will be most beneficial in centers based on the Twelve Step model. Also, people in treatment for codependency may find this book helpful.

Therapists and psychiatrists can use this book and its activities in one-on-one or group settings with clients manifesting behaviors falling into the two main codependency categories: an extreme and often uncontrollable external focus on others coupled with little or no self-awareness, and confusion about their genuine, essential powers and how to use them.

Although not conference approved, this workbook can be used by people who attend any Twelve Step group for codependents, by sponsors working with sponsees, and, with group conscience approval, as part of the Twelve Step meeting. This includes but isn't limited to Al-Anon, CoDA (Co-Dependents Anonymous), ACA (Adult Children of Alcoholics), and Alateen.

The content and activities address "Double Winners"—people affected by codependency and chemical dependency. This workbook also targets people suffering from phobias; fear, panic, or eating disorders; and addictions to sex or gambling. Codependency usually affects people suffering from these problems too. It may be the first or second primary problem they address, but approaching other people's recovery with the adage *Live and let live,* and not insisting that every-one plot a recovery map identical to theirs, will be helpful to all concerned.

"Lifers" attending codependency Twelve Step meetings can benefit from this book and the activities in it, as will people attending meetings as needed. Twelve Step meetings may not be part of some people's recovery protocol, but they can still benefit from the information and activities here, and may discover this work-book helpful in their quest.

People engaged in legitimate caretaking—counselors, nurses, clergy, people caring for ill family members—who attend non-Twelve Step support groups may find this workbook an asset in taking care of themselves.

While reading through the entire workbook may be valuable initially, please follow that by returning to Lesson One, and then completing each lesson and its activities in the order presented. Do the best work possible before moving forward.

The only requirement to benefiting from this book is willingness to openly and honestly do your own work. The book's goal is to assist you in achieving self-love and trust, living your own life, and truly loving others in a way that enhances you and them.

Whether recovering from codependency two days or thirty years, regularly reviewing this workbook and completing the activities will continually reveal fresh insights about letting go, healthy detachment, self-care, and other recovery-related issues.

EDITOR'S NOTE

At the start of each lesson in this workbook, you'll find a quote and a suggested reading from Melody Beattie's classic book *Codependent No More*. These are your links back to pertinent ideas in that book—ideas you can use as a reference and touchstone for working through these lessons.

Before you begin, you will need to purchase a notebook or journal, or create a document on your computer, to use for the activities in this workbook. On page 5 and pages 78–79, where you are asked to fill in some blanks and sign your name, you can simply recreate the relevant text on a separate sheet if you would prefer not to write in this book.

The Stairway to Life

"The Twelve Steps are a way of life."

Matt Speckhart

—Codependent No More

*Suggested reading: "The Twelve Steps" in chapter 18,
"Work a Twelve Step Program"*

In 2001, a friend and I traveled to China on our way to make a pilgrimage around Mount Kailash in Tibet. We changed our plans, deciding to climb four holy mountains in mainland China first. We knew we might not pass that way again.

Mountain climbing in China means climbing thousands and thousands of steps. Once, when the stairway became especially steep, I wondered if I was sure-footed enough to handle it. At that moment, a scrawny man approached and then passed us from behind carrying about seventy-five pounds of wooden beams on his back. The beams were to repair the temple at the mountaintop. Energized by his devotion, I forgot my fears and tackled the steep stairs.

On the longest and hardest climb of all, I began to tire. I had only climbed about halfway up the mountain, but I felt done. Then a group of elderly women who spoke only Chinese surrounded me. Sensing my weariness, one stood in front of me, one behind, and one on each side. The women on my right and left sides each grabbed one of my hands, and we climbed together. Their energy charged through me. It was exactly what I needed to make it to the top. There's magic in groups that have a single-minded purpose.

And we'll get what we need, if we're committed to our path.

When I wondered why I even wanted to climb all these steps, the answer promptly appeared. It was a spiritual quest and a metaphor for recovery.

Your Spiritual Pilgrimage

If we're healing or recovering from codependency, we need to climb up Steps. The difference is, in recovery we don't need to climb thousands of steps. We only need to climb twelve.

Climbing the mountains—or tackling the problems we encounter—continually requires hard work. It can still catch me off guard when, within days of learning a lesson and breathing that trite but welcome breath of relief, a larger, more challenging problem appears. We either experience the same thing over and over until we master the lesson, or one thing after another as new lessons appear, challenging and motivating our spiritual growth.

Change happens in stages, in cycles, or by the pendulum swinging back and forth from extremes until it lands in the sacred, holy middle ground. It surprised many people, including me, to discover that giving up codependent behaviors could take as long as it sometimes does. But if a behavior dominates someone's life for years or decades, change doesn't happen overnight. This kind of transformation can take a long time and requires hard work.

This workbook will be your log and documentation of your spiritual pilgrimage. You'll be taking your lessons directly from the events that have taken place or are happening now in your life. This workbook will provide suggestions on how best to learn and grow from whatever happens to you while you're on your pilgrimage. It will be targeted particularly at what we call *recovering from codependency*.

This workbook, the steps you climb, and the lessons will ask you to look at your life, problems, and relationships in a way that you may not normally do. It will ask you to use the perspective that everything that happens is part of a Greater Plan, one created specifically for you. If you're ready to begin, sign and date your name on the next page to honor the official beginning of your pilgrimage—this part of your journey. It doesn't matter if you're new to recovery and this is your first day, or if you've been recovering for twenty or thirty years. Every day is an opportunity for a new beginning, the start of a new journey, and a chance to use every single thing that occurs for your well-being and growth. You may—for memory's sake—want to include a few notes about how you're feeling, or about various events taking place, to honor the beginning and help you recall this day.

Activity

Sign your name and date this workbook here. Also add a few details about the events taking place in your life and how you feel now.

Signed: *Matt Spacher*

Date: 02/29/2016.

Seperated from my wife.
Beting Dealing with my father
Isues.

Codependency Recovery: A Revolution

When I started working at a drug treatment center in 1975, I wanted to work with the addicts, but the program director assigned me to work with their significant others. The center treated male addicts, so family group consisted of women. We didn't have the word *codependency* yet. We called them *significant others,* but they weren't significant to anyone, including themselves.

"I don't know what to do with them," I told my boss, "and I'm new here."

"Neither do we," he said. "And that's why you get the job."

Nobody else wanted it. The revolution hadn't begun yet.

Although Lois Wilson, Bill Wilson's wife, began Al-Anon meetings in the 1950s, codependency recovery began so quietly then that most of us didn't see it. Bill Wilson wrote the Twelve Steps and cofounded Alcoholics Anonymous (AA). Even in the 1970s, people (I was one) thought Al-Anon was a social event for wives of alcoholics. More treatment centers opened. We knew that people other than old men could be drunks and learned more about addicts. But when it came to the needs of the family, we didn't know what to do, and most people didn't care.

Numerous alcohol and drug treatment centers opened in the 1980s. People working in the field realized treatment and recovery are experimental. Different therapies and techniques could be tried to see what worked.

Diversion became popular, with judges sentencing people convicted of non-violent alcohol or drug crimes to treatment instead of prison. The government and the people felt that alcoholics and addicts deserved another chance. Clearly, addicts and alcoholics can be instrumental in helping each other get sober when clergy, doctors, professors, psychologists, and psychiatrists aren't of much value. Alcoholics and addicts listen to other recovering people, preferring shared experience, strength, hope, role models, and being genuinely understood over college degrees. *If you can do it, I can too* became a powerful transformational belief.

It would take time before these ideas finally evolved into codependency recovery. Sometimes believing creates seeing. In other situations, seeing creates a new belief. Blind faith may not be enough. We have to see somebody like us recover to believe we can.

Significant others continued to know and stay in their place, standing quietly in the backdrop. Treatment centers went through the motions of offering family groups, often because of government regulations. But the results of this therapy weren't impressive. When I attended college to get my degree as a chemical dependency counselor, I received the following training to prepare me for dealing with the family members: "Just listen, nod your head, and agree. Say um-hum," the professor said. "Show empathy."

I did as he instructed, but it didn't work. The training that counselors received was sorely inadequate, but nothing else existed. Like the man carrying the heavy wooden beams up the steep stairway to help rebuild the temple, people will crawl over broken glass—gladly suffer—if they know it's for a good purpose. Later, we learned codependents will sacrifice with or without a purpose. They're happily miserable.

Treatment centers didn't see a purpose to search for the Holy Grail for significant others. What difference would it make? What they needed, at least in Minnesota, was two offensive linemen and a tackle from the Vikings to block the plays made by the significant others when their addicted boyfriend or husband began to get better. Significant others have a finely tuned psychic radar when it comes to what's happening with others, although they're naturally unaware of themselves. When a woman senses changes in her loved one, she'll often try to convince him to leave treatment, even though it might mean he'll end up in jail. She fears that if he gets well, he won't need her. Most people with codependency issues feel genuinely unlovable. They attach themselves to people by caretaking, hoping to become indispensable instead.

"I'd give anything to know what it feels like to be loved," one anonymous recovering woman said. She'd been working on herself for more than twenty years.

As the 1980s rushed in, "name that pain" became the rage. Dysfunctions popped into sight as fast as we could name them. How could we not have seen these problems before—issues such as physical, sexual, and emotional abuse; eating disorders; and compulsive sexual behaviors? Of all the pains named, identifying *codependency* and what needs to be done to heal from it continues to make the greatest positive contribution to the largest number of people's lives.

When I wrote *Codependent No More* in 1986, I thought it might speak to a few people. Instead, hundreds of thousands of people identified themselves as codependents. When awareness and identification of codependency popped into the culture's consciousness, it initially brought excitement and relief. Identifying codependency kicked off a recovery revolution the way nothing else had since AA, Alanon, and NA. We welcomed the explosion.

People enmeshed with addicts, alcoholics, or any kind of dysfunctional family system finally found what they'd been looking for, even if they didn't know they were looking for it. They found validation. They weren't crazy, they were codependent. Given the same set of circumstances, anyone would behave similarly.

Counselors had often felt frustrated with or angry at the family members. The rhetorical buzz questions and phrases among them concerning codependents had become, "They're crazier than the addict or alcoholic," and "Who wouldn't drink with a spouse like that?"

We didn't get the answers to the questions we'd been asking, but when we asked different questions, we got the answers. "Who wouldn't act that crazy after living with an addict or alcoholic?" And, "The addicts and alcoholics medicate pain by drinking and using drugs while the codependents double over with pain, with no medication other than an occasional moment of relief brought on by good old-fashioned denial."

We saw that rarely did a person have an addiction or another compulsive disorder without having codependency. People aren't just chemically dependent. Most are Double Winners—chemically dependent and codependent too.

More and more people recovering from chemical dependency found themselves relapsing or suicidal after about seven years of sobriety, when the repressed pain from codependent behaviors broke through. They needed two Twelve Step recovery programs to create a life that works.

Each of us needs a break from the stark, raving pain of reality once in a while. Some codependents need it every day.

When looked at in the right light, codependency made perfect sense.

Doctors and experts used several terms to describe this condition: *para-alcoholic, nonalcoholic, co-alcoholic. Codependency* is the word that stuck. The word made it into reference books, medical journals, dictionaries, and encyclopedias. The behaviors that accompanied codependency got tagged as *survival behaviors*—behaviors people do to adapt to crazy people and difficult situations.

Survival behaviors are what people do when they don't know what else to do. Survival behaviors aren't preferable, because they begin causing harm to the person using them and to other people. Eventually they can become our downfall, resulting in secondary problems, addictions, or death.

Some people insist that God never gives people more than they can handle. However, the pain can be too great when an eight-year-old is sexually abused, a mother discovers her daughter smoking crack, or a husband learns his wife has been unfaithful since the day they married and the children he thought were theirs aren't his.

Survival behaviors are what people do when they don't have other options for dealing with overwhelming situations. Sometimes survival behaviors are the best we can do. The problem is, these behaviors become habitual. Then, when they turn on us and begin destroying our lives, we don't know how to stop doing them. Without help, we don't have any options.

Changing codependent behaviors became a central part of a huge paradigm shift.

Whenever I heard people say that, I'd nod my head and agree, even though I didn't know what a paradigm was or what happened when it moved. Later I learned it meant a new way of seeing ourselves and the world.

We felt like we discovered fire when codependency recovery began. That's because we did. All those years of repressing emotions and living in denial had numbed and deadened our spirits. Now with recovery, we came alive. We aren't trapped. We don't have to stay stuck in relationships that make us miserable. We're free to choose.

For so many years we thought other people held the key to our happiness. Then we found out we held the key to the prison where we'd been held captive. We might have started out as legitimate victims of others, but then we became victims of ourselves.

Some people became skeptical or cynical about the problems that became named in the 1980s, saying that *dysfunctional* and *family* meant the same thing (which is often true). They called codependency recovery, the art of taking care of ourselves, a symptom of the "Me" generation, but that's not what codependency recovery is. Parents who barely survived the Great Depression or the Holocaust raised and trained the Baby Boomers, the first generation of recovering codependents. Surviving had become a way of life for these parents. That first generation of recovering codependents, like our sometimes severely persecuted parents, became well trained in feeling deprived and undeserving. Codependency recovery counteracts the deprived and undeserving belief systems, but we aren't simply the "Me" generation. It took years of hard work to be able to say, "Me too."

People's attitudes about identifying themselves as codependents dramatically changed in the 1990s. Labeling themselves *codependent* didn't excite or appeal to people anymore. The further away we got from our codependency, the less we wanted to admit that it had been our game. What once brought relief now carried more stigma than admitting to being an addict or alcoholic. I related to this stigma. Being needy, manipulative, or controlling became a source of embarrassment, especially as the public began associating codependency with psychotic, rabbit-boiling stalkers like the borderline personality portrayed by actress Glenn Close in the movie *Fatal Attraction*.

Some recovering people began to manipulate the concept of self-care, turning it into a one-way street to use their emotions to manipulate others while refusing to listen to anyone else's feelings, or crying "abuse" when anyone confronted them. They used their growing knowledge of therapy to justify dysfunctional behaviors, substituting narcissism and self-indulgence for self-love.

Codependents and codependency got a bad reputation. Many people attended Twelve Step groups week after week, year after year, but didn't change. Some got worse. While some people stepped into freedom and connected with true power, others clung to a victim self-image. They didn't want to take responsibility for themselves. They preferred making their pain someone else's fault.

Many people took recovery only partway. They stopped giving compulsively, but didn't learn how to give in healthy ways. They became afraid to love, care for, and nurture people, which were all important parts of a healthy life. Some insisted they'd be sick all their lives, instead of allowing themselves to develop a healthy self-image. Other people blatantly insisted everyone had to attend meetings all their lives for codependency, when that isn't true. Some people may only need to attend groups for a while, some intermittently, some all their lives, and some may not need to attend Twelve Step meetings at all. This isn't a one-size-fits-all problem or solution.

Attendance at some groups, especially the unhealthy ones, dwindled while other groups worked hard to stay healthy and on track. New kinds of support groups sprang up, offering support for people involved in legitimate caretaking to help them remember to take care of themselves. They didn't need Twelve Step meetings, but they could use some encouragement and support.

By then, computers had become standard fixtures in most people's homes. After the millennium, people easily attended support groups or Step meetings online.

But many people tired of working on themselves. They thought initially it might take a few months to change. Then they discovered it could take decades to let go of habitual patterns. Added to that was that dealing with feelings became more dangerous than opening Pandora's box. In Pandora's box, everything is gone except hope. There was no hope for an ending to emotions. As soon as we feel one, another one, two, or three more emotions appear.

People became confused about codependency. Two people can do the same behavior, but in one person the behavior is codependent, and in the other person the behavior is a healthy choice. People wanted clear rules to determine what's codependent and what's not, instead of having to trust themselves. But it's not the external behaviors that determine codependency. The test for what's codependent is *What's the motivation for what you're doing?* Are you doing something because you made a conscious choice to do it, or are you acting from guilt and obligation? Are you choosing to give or giving compulsively without thinking about what you're doing? Are you hoping someone will like or love you if you do something for, or give something to, her or him? Do you feel lovable and likable, and have self-esteem? Or do you have to prove those things to other people and yourself? How do you feel when you're done doing the behavior? Do you feel resentful, used, and victimized? Or do you feel comfortable with and responsible for your choices?

Many factors caused people to become disillusioned with recovery, but the biggest reason that people don't get what they can out of recovery is that many codependents do not work the Twelve Steps. Most recovering addicts attend Twelve Step meetings and work the Steps as if their lives depend on it, because their lives do. Often, codependents don't apply the recovery principles to their lives to replace codependent behaviors and reactions.

People can go to groups, talk recovery talk, but continue to stay stuck in their sighing, victimized codependent ways. People may know how to sound therapeutically correct. They know the right things to say. But their behaviors do not match their words.

Instead of learning to trust themselves, groups and people in recovery wanted rules. Some groups became as repressive and dysfunctional as the family systems that originally helped people develop codependency, operating by the same unhealthy rules: *Don't think, don't feel, don't be who you are, don't trust yourself.* Some people stopped taking codependency recovery seriously, calling it the popular "illness of the week."

But codependency recovery—whether it involves an alcoholic or addicted person or not—is more than a trend. It helps people get and keep a life. Sometimes it saves their lives too.

Activity

Write about your experience with attending groups of any kind and attending Twelve Step groups for codependency recovery. Write about what you've worked on, a short history of your recovery, and your work with the Steps. Also include any progress, detailing particular behaviors or improvements you've made.

Saving Your Life

What many people with codependency issues don't understand is that their lives depend on them working the Steps. They deserve to heal from their pain just as much as alcoholics and addicts do. If they earnestly begin working the Steps—and in many cases *only* if they work the Steps—they'll heal too.

We no longer have only first-generation codependents recovering. Now we have multiple generations of people displaying codependent behaviors. Many people show signs of classic codependency, no matter what generation they're in: people-pleasing, caretaking, controlling, lack of boundaries, and believing they're deprived and undeserving.

But many people now demonstrate a mutated form of codependency. *Deprived* and *undeserving* don't describe them. They feel entitled to everything, whether they work for it or not. It's the other side of the coin. They'd been overprotected and overindulged. I've repeatedly had people contact me after a therapist or friend suggested they read *Codependent No More*. "I'm in pain, all messed up. I need to talk to you right away," they insist.

They don't ask. They impatiently demand my attention.

They may have been coddled for many years, but they can't hide forever. One by one, reality is finding them. But they write to me, expecting me to give them a way to solve their problem and heal their discomfort in less than a day.

Frequently, when I get these urgent, demanding messages from people who moan they can't take the way they're feeling one more second, I'll ask: "What have you done so far today to take care of yourself? What Steps have you worked? Have you written in your journal, exercised, prayed, or meditated?" The e-mails cease, replaced by silence. "I'll talk to you," I write. "But not until you do at least three self-care behaviors first."

That's when the person quietly slips away. I don't have a magic wand. Neither does anyone else.

In the 1990s, instead of calling themselves *codependent,* many people avoided the word and talked about their behaviors as if they were individual, disconnected problems. "I have anxiety and depression." "I'm an agoraphobic, and I feel depressed." "I have panic attacks." "I'm full of fear." The use of antidepressants and antianxiety medications became popular. Some people certainly do need medications for mental health issues, but I do ask people to consider how they might be able to take better care of themselves if they became sincerely involved in a Twelve Step program. If you have been taking medication, it is critical to *not* stop taking it unless it's under a doctor's guidance and care. If you have questions about whether your medication should be continued, talk to your doctor and work closely with him or her in making a decision.

I've been saying this for more than thirty years to people, because someone cared enough to teach me: *Being happy means surrendering to and feeling all our feelings, not just feeling happy.* It means being at peace with whatever is and how we feel—angry, upset, sad—each moment in time.

Working the Steps usually leads to doing other recovery work, such as family-of-origin work, going to therapy, or focusing on changing a particular behavior, but the force that moves us forward in recovery, that causes us to go against gravity by going up, not down, has been, is, and likely will continue to be, for most people, working the Steps. Learning these principles and applying them can even benefit people who don't attend Twelve Step groups.

Alcoholism is described as cunning, baffling, and powerful. But those words describe codependency too. Codependency can be absolutely and totally exhausting. It drains and depletes people, puts a blindfold on them, spins them around in circles until they're dizzy. Then people try to go on with their lives and wonder why they can't.

You're not crazy. Codependency can make you feel crazy, though. When you look at yourself with eyes of love instead of criticism, you'll see that everything happens for a reason, including what you do. Your codependent behaviors make perfect sense. Your goal was to survive. You did. Now, by working the Steps, first by going through them in depth, and then by using them as daily life tools, you'll begin to thrive.

Here are the Twelve Steps used by Co-Dependents Anonymous, based on the original Twelve Steps of Alcoholics Anonymous, but with slight changes suggested for people who want to create healthy relationships:

TWELVE STEPS OF
CO-DEPENDENTS ANONYMOUS

1. We admitted we were powerless over others—that our lives had become unmanageable.

2. Came to believe that a power greater than ourselves could restore us to sanity.

3. Made a decision to turn our will and lives over to the care of God as we understood God.

4. Made a searching and fearless moral inventory of ourselves.

5. Admitted to God, to ourselves, and to another human being, the exact nature of our wrongs.

6. Were entirely ready to have God remove all these defects of character.

7. Humbly asked God to remove our shortcomings.

8. Made a list of all persons we had harmed and became willing to make amends to them all.

9. Made direct amends to such people wherever possible, except when to do so would injure them or others.

10. Continued to take personal inventory and when we were wrong, promptly admitted it.

11. Sought through prayer and meditation to improve our conscious contact with God as we understood God, praying only for knowledge of God's will for us and the power to carry that out.

12. Having had a spiritual awakening as the result of these steps, we tried to carry this message to other co-dependents, and to practice these principles in all our affairs.

The Steps are the heart of recovery and this book.

Working the Twelve Steps is how we heal from the different ways codependency hurt and affected us, whether they're the Twelve Steps of Al-Anon (those affected by another person's drinking), Co-Dependents Anonymous (people whose behaviors negatively affect their relationships), Codependents of Sex Addicts (people affected by another person's compulsive sexual behavior), Gam-Anon (people affected by someone's compulsive gambling), or Nar-Anon (people affected by someone using drugs).

These Steps, or suggested principles for living, will help you replace learned habitual survival behaviors with healthy options that in time will become a new way of life. By working the Steps, you become transformed. But you still have work to do. While the Steps are the means to transformation, they also lead to other activities that bring the specific types of healing each person requires. That might include becoming aware of and changing negative or limiting beliefs, seeing a therapist, attending groups, reading a book, or doing any of many different activities that bring exactly what you need to heal at the right time.

As they say in Twelve Step meetings, *Keep an open mind.*

Activity

1 At the end of this workbook, you'll find several versions of these Steps. Each version, whether for Al-Anon, Gam-Anon, or Co-Dependents Anonymous, has only slight variations—but these variations might be important to you. Read through the different versions. Pick one that appeals to you. Write or type out a copy to carry in your wallet or purse. Don't worry about whether you're making the right choice about which version to use. You can always redecide.

2 If you're new to recovery, read through the Steps daily for the next three months. If you've been recovering for up to three years, read through them weekly; if you've been recovering three to five years, monthly; and if you've been recovering five years or more, you'll know how often to review the Steps. If you're working a program, you can trust yourself. But it will benefit you even after decades of recovery to read through them at least three times a year.

Getting Back What You Give

Some people don't understand the concept of *doing their recovery work for themselves.* They think that the key to their change is something that a therapist, group leader, treatment center, or book holds. While the Steps may lead us to do certain activities that help, the magic only happens when a person does his or her own work by digging deeply inside him- or herself.

Whether we're talking about a career, a relationship, or our recovery, we get what we want by investing our time and energy, and by giving of ourselves. The Baby Boomer codependents are becoming aware that because people live longer now, they need to continue recreating their lives instead of passively waiting for whatever comes.

"I read *Codependent No More* over twenty years ago, when it first came out," a woman said. "Recently, I took it out. It's time to read and remember it again."

You're wiser than you think. You don't need rules. Forget about therapeutic correctness. You'll know if codependency is an issue that's affecting you. You'll also know which behaviors to work on, which Steps to work, and when. If you don't, ask yourself or your Higher Power what to do and when to do it. That behavior—asking for guidance—is one of the Steps.

One behavior leads into and helps create another. We're either getting better or, because codependency is progressive, getting worse. Whether we're creating a downward or upward spiral of recovery is up to us.

If we've worked on our codependent behaviors for a while, they may be more subtle than in the beginning, but they can still cause pain. Our controlling and manipulation may be more refined. We may not know how much we're repressing until we begin consciously working on becoming aware of our emotions, either for the first time or again.

If we've been recovering for a while, we may have raised the bar to what we'll tolerate as an acceptable level of sanity and serenity in our lives. The level of drama we lived with before may not be appropriate for us now. Setting limits and creating a recovery plan is up to us.

The bottom line is, we get out of anything what we put into it. If we want a life that works, one that is interesting and real, one that we're passionate about, then we need to get out of our numb, passive state and put energy into self-care. We need to do the work, and that includes working the Steps.

They're the stairs that lead to life.

Activity

1. Ask yourself these questions, and then answer honestly. Work with the affirmations that follow them, as instructed, until the answer to each question is an unreserved yes.

   - Are you willing to feel uncomfortable at times, when you grow and change?

   - Are you willing to feel emotions, including pain and fear? Many therapists agree that if a behavior doesn't feel uncomfortable, and we don't feel fearful about doing it, it means we're not doing anything new. It's the same old thing.

   - Are you willing to work the Steps both ways—by working through them at least once, thoroughly, and then learning to use them as daily living tools?

   - Are you willing to work hard on yourself, possibly for a long time—as long as it takes to recover "full circle" or completely?

2. Read the following affirmations at least twice a day. At least once daily, read them out loud. Consider photocopying them and carrying them with you as a reminder of your commitment to recovery and yourself.

Activity (cont.)

I'm okay with being uncomfortable and sometimes feeling emotional pain as part of my healing process. I'm committed to continuing with my recovery despite how I feel and any uncomfortable emotions that come up.

I'm willing to feel all my feelings, understanding that surrendering to, feeling, and then releasing them is what true happiness is.

I'm okay with taking as much time as I need to change any behaviors and replace them with healthy options that help me love and take care of myself.

I'm okay with letting go of my old survival behaviors. I don't need them now. I'm okay with acquiring and practicing new behaviors that will help me address challenges, issues, and problems in a new way, one that helps me thrive.

I understand that I'm not being singled out or picked on because of the problems, lessons, and challenges that appear on my path or by having emotions I need to feel. I know and trust I'm being shaped into a healthy person who understands the meaning of true happiness and knows how to love others and myself.

I understand that the way to getting and keeping a life is by working the Twelve Steps, first going through them slowly and thoroughly, then later using them as daily living tools.

Activity (cont.)

Activity (cont.)

I understand that changing can require hard work, and it's work that I need to do myself. I'm willing to work as hard as needed.

I'll put as much energy into doing the work it takes to change as I've put into hanging onto old unhealthy ways. I know if I do that I'll succeed. I also understand and am okay with the idea that I can't do the work for anyone besides me.

My recovery and self-care is my responsibility and my job.

It's okay to put my well-being first sometimes. I won't get hooked into perfectionism but I'll do my best. When I've done that, I'll let go and let God do the rest.

I'm willing to stay with recovery until I can give in healthy ways, love and nurture others and myself, and completely release a victim self-image.

When you feel like you understand to the best of your ability the information in this lesson, and you can read the affirmations without feeling any resistance, you're ready to move forward to the next lesson. Listen to and trust yourself, and you'll know when it's time. This is an experiential workbook. The act of going through it and making choices is part of the healing process itself.

Now, put down the workbook. Go out and do something you want to do. Work hard, pray hard, and learn to have fun.

Recognizing Your Teachers

"*Another reason codependency is called a disease*

is because it is progressive.

As the people around us become sicker,

we may begin to react more intensely."

Mart Sprahw

—Codependent No More

Suggested reading: "A Brief History" in chapter 3, "Codependency"

STEP ONE: We admitted we were powerless over others—that our lives had become unmanageable.

—from the TWELVE STEPS OF CO-DEPENDENTS ANONYMOUS

The exact wording of this Step changes slightly from program to program. We can also change it in our head if we need to, so it makes sense and applies to whatever person, substance, or behavior we're trying unsuccessfully to control.

Taking the First Step to Your Destination

Fill in the blank below so it relates to your current situation and makes sense to you.

We admitted we were powerless over ___Codependency___
—*that our lives had become unmanageable.*

Here's one Double Winner's story of how she worked Step One. Respecting the anonymity tradition of Twelve Step programs, I'm leaving out the name. It's the experience that matters. Try to let down your guard and any resistance that arises. *Don't look for the differences, look for the similarities,* suggests one Twelve Step saying. Look for what you have in common with the people whose stories you'll read throughout this book.

"THE LEGAL SYSTEM ORDERED my first exposure to the Twelve Steps. I'd been using alcohol and drugs since age twelve. Looking back, I was a full-blown alcoholic by the time I turned thirteen. I blacked out, lost control of when I drank, how much I drank, and what I did when I drank. During blackouts, I'd walk, talk, and look as if I were fully conscious. But the next day, I couldn't recall anything about what happened. I didn't know who I'd been with, but even worse, I didn't know what I'd done. One thing I knew: What I did wasn't good. I became filled with shame and remorse.

"I switched to drugs when I turned seventeen. I used and then abused pills, then cocaine, morphine, heroin. At first I refused to shoot drugs. Within a year, if I could get it into a syringe, I'd shove it into my veins. Despite alcoholism and addiction, I graduated on the City Honor Roll. The world didn't know much about addiction and alcoholism then. Everyone, including me, knew something was wrong with me. But nobody could name my problem or tell me how to solve it. They said I should straighten up and behave. What they and I didn't know is that not only did I not know how—I had already completely lost control.

"I hadn't told anyone that I'd been repeatedly sexually abused since age eleven. I didn't understand sexual abuse, or what it meant. I knew men that I should have been able to trust did things to me that made me feel badly about myself, but I didn't have anyone I could talk to about it. I didn't know how to communicate. Besides, I thought I brought it on myself.

"My mom had divorced my dad when I was a toddler. My brother and sisters, all older than I am, ran away long ago, escaped, moved out of the house. I had watched family members physically abuse them. The scenes horrified me then. They still do now when I remember them. I escaped physical abuse because of heart problems. As a baby, I spent a year in the hospital. During grade school, doctors ordered me to bed rest for a year. Then the doctors confined me to bed again for a year during high school. Totally removing me from all social contact negatively impacted the few social skills I had.

"I didn't know how to talk to people. I didn't have friends. I didn't understand feelings. All I knew was that I didn't feel good unless I drank or used drugs. Alcohol made me feel warm and good enough. Drugs made me feel more peaceful about being alive. Drugs soon became my reason to live. From hearing my mother say that she should have aborted me, and because of the other harmful incidents that happened to me, I concluded that I should never have been born. I didn't have the courage to commit suicide, although I made a few attempts. But I knew if I kept using drugs the way I did, I wouldn't live a long life.

"After many arrests for possession of narcotics, a judge sentenced me to treatment when I was in my early twenties. By then, I didn't have any veins left. Shooting drugs had become hard work. I became confined by state order to a state hospital's chemical dependency treatment unit. The program consisted of a community group who visited the hospital weekly to put on an AA meeting. I also attended morning lectures, a weekly one-hour session with my counselor, and a weekly therapy group where we were supposed to talk about our feelings.

"During the AA meetings, I made fun of the recovering alcoholics. The posters they set up on the stage were the same posters tacked on the walls in my cottage. They listed something called the Twelve Steps of Alcoholics Anonymous. I didn't have a clue what these Steps were talking about.

"All I knew is that I wanted to get high, and I did whenever I could even though I was in treatment, and if I got caught I would be sent to prison for up to five years. Although I'd overdosed and almost died four times, I thought I controlled my drug using. I believed I chose to get high. Before the last arrest—the one that resulted in the judge ordering me to treatment—I'd been burglarizing drugstores with my boyfriend. I didn't see any of my behaviors as crazy. Everything I did made sense to me.

"Treatment slowed down my use of drugs. I either drank or used drugs daily before going there. Now I was lucky if I could get alcohol or drugs once or twice a week. Then what I got wasn't much or very good. The stupor I'd been in for twelve years slowly began to lift. Something began changing inside me. Looking back, I can see now that I began feeling again. I was coming back to life.

"About three months into treatment, my probation officer called and said he'd be there early the next morning. Shortly after he called, I scored some speed. They were the strongest drugs I'd been able to get since getting there. I got enough to keep me high for a week, and I had enough sense to realize I shouldn't use anything until after my probation officer left the next morning. Not only had I begun feeling again, a small amount of rational thought returned.

"I went to bed about nine that night after hiding the drugs in my closet. I couldn't fall asleep. The drugs kept calling my name. Finally I took one pill and went back to bed. *How stupid,* I thought. *One pill won't do any good.* I took another one. Fifteen minutes later, I took two more. By midnight I'd taken every pill I had. I couldn't stop myself. Then I laid there bug-eyed, amped on amphetamines. I watched the hands on the clock spin around. By six a.m., I hadn't closed my eyes. Now it was time to get up. My probation officer would soon arrive.

"I felt terrified of getting caught. *What was I thinking of? I could go to jail for this,* I thought. *I'm not controlling drugs. They're controlling me.* For the first time since I started drinking and using drugs, I saw the truth. If I took one pill, I couldn't stop using drugs until they were completely gone.

"The first words on those posters ran through my mind. *I'm powerless over alcohol and drugs and my life is unmanageable.* Now I understood. This Step described me and my loss of control.

"I made it through the meeting with my probation officer without getting caught, but I still felt overwhelmed with fear. For the first time ever, I wanted to stop drinking and using drugs, but I didn't know how to stop. I hadn't prayed in years, since I had started drinking. But as soon as my probation officer left, I looked at the ceiling. 'God, I don't know if You're there and You care,' I whispered. 'But if You are and You do, and if there's a program that will help me stop using, please help me get it. Thank You. Amen.'

"Nothing happened. I felt helpless, hopeless, and depressed. I didn't know what to do, and I didn't want to go to prison. Three days later, someone handed me a joint—marijuana. I couldn't say no. I went outside to smoke it. Instead of getting high, something strange happened. I didn't just feel God's presence. I knew He was real. Instead of feeling entitled to getting high, I knew I had no right to keep doing what I'd been doing. *If I put half as much energy into doing the right thing as I've put into getting high, there isn't much I can't do,* I thought, taking one more hit off the joint. I snuffed it out, and then went inside the cottage and hurled myself into recovery with all the passion I'd put into getting high.

"I used once more in treatment, at a party. When someone handed me a bottle of whiskey, I automatically lifted the bottle to my lips and took a drink. Something strange happened again. Instead of getting that usual warm feeling in my stomach, I felt overwhelmed with guilt. I felt so guilty that in group the next day I told my counselor what I'd done, even though telling the truth could send me to prison. I hadn't had a conscience for years.

"I confessed, and with deep remorse, said I knew I had to begin my sobriety over. I felt worse about that than I did about the possibility of going to jail. My counselor asked if I'd learned anything from what I did. I said I learned that I couldn't go around people who were using or drinking because if I did, I'd have a slip. I'd relapse and begin using again. Besides, something had ruined my using. I didn't feel high. I felt guilt.

"'Then what you did doesn't sound like a mistake,' my counselor said. 'It sounds like you learned an important lesson. You don't need to start over,' she said. 'Keep moving forward.' Thank God for that woman. She helped change the course of my life.

"It excites me now to look back at when I 'got' the First Step, but at the time I didn't feel excited. I felt depressed. Now I understand that I needed to feel that way before I could go where I went next. Those feelings prepared me. Taking the First Step meant moving out of denial and finally telling the truth to myself about what using alcohol and drugs did to my life."

Double Winners Admit They're Powerless Over Other People Too

Surrender is something that hurts until we do it. It can feel scary. Then doing what we feared neutralizes the pain. Here's the rest of the above story about the alcoholic and addict who took her First Step.

"I HAD TO WORK THE FIRST FIVE STEPS before leaving treatment. But working the Steps turned from something I had to do into something I wanted to do. The Twelve Steps were God's answer to my prayer. I quickly learned if I did the best I could to work each Step, that was good enough.

"Depression began to lift. When I saw that God heard and answered my prayer, it showed me that God cared, that I wasn't alone like I'd always felt I was. I'd attended church until I became a junkie, but I'd never experienced what I found in treatment. Alcoholics Anonymous calls it *a personal relationship with God.* I call it *a spiritual experience.*

"Twelve Step programs have many sayings and slogans that can be as helpful as the Steps, but some seem unrealistic. One says, 'Don't have a relationship for the first one or two years of sobriety.' But almost everyone breaks that rule, and then they feel guilty about it.

"I waited two years and then married a man also recovering from chemical dependency, only he'd been recovering a lot longer than me. He hadn't used drugs. He preferred alcohol. He expressed concern about me using drugs again—having a slip. But then he said he loved me and would take a chance on me. I adored him. A mutual friend in recovery had introduced us. It became love at first sight. I didn't know how to date. My experiences with the opposite sex consisted of older men sexually abusing me and relationships with drug addicts— relationships built around a common desire to get high.

"A month after we married, I became pregnant. I was thrilled. I'd lay awake at night, hardly able to take in how much God had blessed me. The one thing I wanted was a loving family. Now I had that. This made everything I'd gone through worthwhile. My husband and I had a slight problem on our honeymoon. His father had died. My husband went out and didn't come home until six the next morning. I wanted to comfort him, but he wouldn't let me. He didn't even let me go to the funeral with him.

"I didn't know what love and a good marriage looked like. My brother and sisters had a different biological father than I did. I came along late in my mother's life, just when she got close to being free from raising children. Her first husband died. She raised us by herself. When the other kids left home, she was done being a parent. She left in the morning for work and didn't return until late at night. Besides her day job, she usually ran a business on the side that kept her busy every evening. She could handle money, but she couldn't handle me. 'You're just like your father,' she said. 'He's a good-for-nothing alcoholic.'

"I didn't know my dad. When I turned three, he said, 'Okay for you.' Then he left and remarried. I saw him only a few times after that. He had two more children. He loved his new family, but it didn't include me.

"When I started drinking, I thought he'd be proud of me for taking after him. But when I became a teenager and stopped by his house one day and asked him for a beer, he became angry. I left feeling confused. I didn't know who to be or who I was. Nothing I did pleased my mother, and who I was didn't please my father.

"After my husband stayed out all night during our honeymoon, things got worse instead of better. Frequently he'd disappear. I didn't feel close to him. We rarely talked about anything important although we both felt excited that I'd become pregnant.

"Then on a Saturday, shortly after I gave birth to our daughter, the water in the toilet wouldn't stop running. I tried to fix it by jiggling the handle, but that didn't help. Finally I lifted up the tank cover. When I did, I discovered the problem with the toilet and our marriage. My husband had stashed a half-empty bottle of vodka in the tank. *Classic,* I thought, feeling shocked. Suddenly, everything made sense. All the times he disappeared and couldn't be found, all the days he'd lay in bed claiming he didn't sleep the night before, he'd really been drinking. More than anything, his drinking and lying about it explained the separation from him I'd felt since the day we married.

"When I confronted him about the vodka bottle, he said he had a slip. He asked for my forgiveness. This started a pattern that dominated our marriage. Only usually he'd drink and then lie about it. I'd try to catch him, playing the sobriety police.

"The night I found the vodka bottle in the toilet I grabbed our daughter and drove around town until the middle of the night. All I could do was cry. I didn't understand how God could let this happen. I thought my marriage was a gift from God. Some gift! But if I admitted that I married an alcoholic, I'd have to get divorced; otherwise it could jeopardize my sobriety. The only answer I could see was to make him stop drinking. I didn't know what felt worse, the betrayal I felt from my husband or the betrayal I felt from God. I felt totally abandoned by the God who had shown me so much love in treatment.

"I spent the next seven years doing everything I could think of—and more—to make my husband stop drinking. Besides the drinking, I knew in my gut that he'd become involved with another woman.

But I couldn't catch him, and he denied cheating. I couldn't validate my feelings, and that drove me crazy. Every Sunday he'd leave in the morning to get a newspaper, and he wouldn't return until late that afternoon. When I asked him where he'd been, he said all the stores had sold out of the paper, and he had to drive all over town to find one. He said the same thing every week. We both knew that I knew he was lying. But if I accused him of drinking or having an affair, he called me suspicious and crazy. Sometimes I'd hear him bragging on the phone to his friends about how some things you had to take to the grave, but if you didn't admit it, then nobody could prove it.

"I constantly felt this anxiety in the pit of my stomach. It drove me to dig through the pockets in his jackets, his pants. Constantly I searched for clues, for evidence, anything to confirm my suspicions. If I caught him in the act of adultery, I'd have the reason I needed to file for divorce. Before I found any evidence, I became pregnant again.

"Despite our marital problems, being pregnant thrilled me. But our home life got crazier. His alcoholism continued to progress and cause problems. I kept trying to deny that he was an alcoholic. He lost jobs, one after another. Then he began borrowing thousands of dollars to invest in ridiculous get-rich-quick schemes so he wouldn't have to work. I lost all respect for him. He constantly bounced checks. He couldn't handle money. I couldn't leave him alone with the children for two hours. His touch made my skin crawl. I no longer felt blessed by this marriage. I felt trapped.

"I kept threatening to leave him, but he didn't listen. Who could blame him? I didn't listen to myself. He didn't attend AA, except for one meeting he said he went to so I'd stop nagging. When he came home and I asked about the meeting, he said the focus had been on how a nagging wife could make her husband keep drinking. I felt guilty, but that was how I usually felt. Years later he admitted he hadn't even gone to a meeting.

"He lied to me for seven years about his drinking. I spent seven years lying to myself.

"What made me think I could control him? As a recovering addict and alcoholic myself, I knew an alcoholic loses control. How could I possibly control someone who couldn't control himself? Alcohol had gained control of me again, but this time it controlled me through someone else's drinking.

"I spent hours complaining about my husband to my neighbor. I'd sit in her kitchen and obsess. Usually she listened. But one day when I told her about the latest stunt I'd done to show him how much his lying and drinking hurt me, she spoke up. 'You're acting crazy,' she said. 'Yes, he's an alcoholic, but your behavior is so out of control it's scaring me more than his is. You need to go to Al-Anon meetings.'

"What I'd done this time had been so bizarre that to this day I haven't told anyone about it, except in my Fifth Step. Still I became angry when she said I needed meetings. I'd stayed sober. I held the family together. Why should I be the one to get help when he had the problem?

"Finally, I became suicidal, so depressed and obsessed with my husband that I couldn't even take the children to the park. I rarely left the house, afraid he might drink if I did. Anger controlled my every behavior, but I didn't have any awareness of what I felt. Finally I gave in and went to my first Al-Anon meeting, but only because I had nowhere else to go. When I explained I was a recovering alcoholic and addict, a woman called me a Double Winner. That made me mad. I hadn't won anything. I only saw what I'd lost: my dream of a loving family, my marriage, and my desire to live. I lost all trust in and respect for my husband. Most of all, somewhere along the line I'd lost myself.

"When the meeting started and people began talking about the pain they felt watching someone they love destroying themselves and their marriage by drinking, I started crying.

"Crying felt good. It was a legitimate feeling, something besides the bitterness, nagging, and anger. Spending seven years trying to do the impossible had left me exhausted, depleted, worn out. I didn't want to be at that meeting. I thought Al-Anon was like a ladies' aid society.

But these people who talked about their lives told my story too. Plus, they looked happy. Serene. They'd found a way to be at peace with themselves, the other person, and life, regardless of what the other person did.

"I surrendered. As tears ran down my face from feeling the first feeling besides rage that I'd felt in years, I admitted to myself and to everyone in that room that I was powerless over my husband's drinking and my life had become unmanageable.

"At last I became ready to face the truth."

A New Perspective

As this woman's story concludes, we see how she is now able to face her control issues and finally work an effective Twelve Step program.

"I HONESTLY THOUGHT that surrendering to the truth and letting go of trying to control my husband would be the only time I'd need to detach from trying to control someone. That couldn't have been further from the truth. It began the process of me learning a new behavior and reframing reality. I grew up with an extraordinarily controlling mother. I'm not blaming my behavior on her. I grew up in an era that accepted control as normal. Society believed that people should control their spouse, their children, and themselves. I didn't have a dysfunctional relationship only with my husband. I had a dysfunctional relationship with control. I didn't know the difference between what I couldn't control and what I could. My first and instinctive reaction to almost everything that happened that I didn't like? I tried to control it.

"Years later I saw my husband as my teacher. He taught me about letting ago.

"He never did stop drinking, at least not for long. After I divorced him, his drinking got worse. Eventually he died at age fifty-eight from an alcohol-related incident. Although I didn't get my dream of a loving family, I consider myself blessed. I had two beautiful children, and when I admitted the truth about what I couldn't control, I began a loving relationship with myself and a realistic relationship with power and control.

"I began to work the Twelve Steps for the second time. Gradually I understood what it meant to be a Double Winner. I had won twice. First I received the gift of sobriety. Then, instead of spending every waking moment obsessing about my husband, I began taking care of myself and my responsibilities. God didn't abandon me. I abandoned myself. I began to learn for the first time in my life what it meant to take care of myself. I got my life back."

The Twelve Steps are powerful tools. Some require action. Some require a new way of thinking. We need to work the Steps, but when we reach out to them, they meet us halfway. The Steps start working us.

Activity

1. Is there someone in your life who's come to teach you something? Who? You may not understand the lesson yet. We usually don't until later, in retrospect, after we master the lesson. When a problem arises, try to remember that life is a classroom and any person you're having difficulty with is a teacher. Then keep an open mind. Let yourself go through the experience and learn the lesson.

2. Make and continue adding to a list of your teachers and the lessons you learn, especially the hard lessons, when you didn't know you were going to be learning something. Find as many teachers and lessons from your past as you can. Know that you'll likely be learning and growing the rest of your life.

3. Learning doesn't always have to spring from difficulty, pain, and opposition. Include on your list the teachers who taught without pain or situations where you didn't have to learn the hard way, and what you learned from that.

Control as a Reaction to Loss

It's not crazy to want to save your marriage. Just because you begin working the Steps doesn't mean you need to file for divorce. Two people can do the same behavior, and for one, it's a sign of codependency, and for the other, it's a healthy choice. You can leave someone for all the wrong reasons, and it won't help your healing process or advance your growth. Or you can end a relationship as a healthy decision that advances your spiritual growth.

"I spent years worrying about whether our marriage would work or not," the woman in the above story said. "I later learned that worrying is also a form of control. The problem is that control doesn't work. One day I realized the time had come to end our marriage. I felt clear, no confusion. I didn't have to force the decision or make anything happen. The longer I work the Twelve Steps, the more I realize I can't control things and I don't have to," she said.

"Al-Anon and working its Twelve Steps reprogrammed me. There's a new program in my head that clicks off the facts, reality. I evaluate the situation and decide what I can control and what I can't. Although I still get sucked into trying to control certain situations, especially when they involve accepting a loss, I usually catch myself when I start controlling. Then I detach."

Working the First Step can be the appropriate response to many situations that we'd otherwise try to control. Most of those situations involve losing something or someone important. Losing a relationship, admitting that someone we love has a serious problem or illness, or losing our health are three common loss situations that can trigger our need to control.

It can be heartbreaking to lose a family member to alcoholism or addiction. It can feel good to take Step One even when we're hurting. It validates us when we finally surrender to the truth. All the time we spend searching through someone's pockets, looking in his or her day planner, or trying to catch him or her doing a behavior we know in our heart that person is doing, we're actually trying to validate ourselves. It's crazy-making to believe lies, or to know the truth at a deep level and consistently be lied to about it. *The truth shall set you free* is an ancient saying and a recovery slogan.

We can stop waiting for someone else to tell us we're not crazy. We can take the First Step and validate ourselves.

Obsessively focusing on other people while remaining oblivious to our behaviors is another symptom of codependency. Becoming and staying aware of ourselves takes intention, discipline, and practice. When we believe lies and obsess about other people, we lose touch with ourselves, our emotions, and our intuition. We lose touch with what we know is true. Here's the rest of the Double Winner's story and a happier ending.

"Many years later, the principal at the high school I attended asked me to come back and talk to the students about alcoholism and drug addiction. I hated myself so much as a child and teenager that I'd destroyed all pictures of me. Because the principal wanted to surprise me, he managed to find the one picture that existed of me in my teenage years. Before I began my speech, he flashed this larger-than-life photo of me on the auditorium wall. I looked at myself and saw a picture of a teenage girl who looked so dark, so depressed, so burdened. My heart went out to her. You could see how much she hurt. Seeing that picture threw me off balance. It took everything I had to calmly give my speech.

"That began a process of months of healing from feelings I'd repressed from my childhood and teenage years. I'd felt lost and despised by everyone. I felt so ugly, unwanted, and unlovable. I despised myself. All these emotions tumbled into consciousness.

"I could barely handle these feelings as an adult. No way could I have handled them as a child, especially without help. I believe that medicating my feelings by drinking and using drugs kept me from committing suicide, something I thought about a lot as a child. Alcoholism and addiction can kill us, but in a strange way, it saved my life. I had tried to deal with the emotionally overwhelming situation of sexual abuse and life in a crazy family the only way I knew—by drinking and using drugs.

"Now I could stop judging myself and thinking of myself as a bad person for being an alcoholic and an addict. If I felt as a child the way I did for five months after giving that talk, it's a miracle that I didn't kill myself when I was a child."

Recovery comes in layers. We peel away one problem, and underneath it we find another. Often we address these problems in the reverse order they appeared. The problem that developed last is the one we address first. But there's no set rule for it, and we're each unique.

Codependency isn't minor. It's a major problem, and it can be deadly. Even if we don't die or kill ourselves, we can feel like the living dead. At first, people attending fundamentalist Alcoholics Anonymous meetings didn't want to acknowledge that many recovering alcoholics had codependent behaviors underneath alcoholism. But many of them felt miserable to the point of being suicidal after becoming sober. Things change. Now many cities offer dual disorder or Double Winner groups. People can go to one meeting and work two Twelve Step programs. Or they can take one First Step that includes powerlessness over both alcoholism and codependent behaviors.

Surrendering to the truth hurts; otherwise we wouldn't need to deny reality as long as so many of us do. But recovery means surrendering to divine timing. We'll stop lying to ourselves when we're strong enough to face the truth.

When I began researching and learning about codependency, I had a difficult time understanding the denial part. How could so many intelligent, educated, capable people spend so much of their lives denying reality? Then I found the writings of Dr. Elisabeth Kübler-Ross. She identified the five stages of dying that later became known as the five stages of loss and grief: denial, anger, bargaining, depression, and acceptance. I would add two more to the list: guilt and obsession. Much of what causes codependency is people becoming stuck in a stage of grief, and then making that stuck behavior a way of life.

When denial runs our life, it's because we're facing the loss of something we're not prepared to lose. For example, losing our marriage and all the dreams that accompany it is a major loss, not something that comes easy. Facing it can create a lot of grief. It's normal to want to control the loss, or make whatever's happening stop taking place. Codependent behaviors are normal, instinctive responses to certain events. Usually those events involve loss. Recovery often means learning to do the opposite of what we think we should do. For instance, instead of trying to make a person stop drinking so we don't lose our marriage, we learn to let go, detach with love, and take care of ourselves.

It's natural to want to keep someone we love in our lives. It's natural to want the people we love to be healthy. We don't want them to have serious problems. It's normal to want ourselves to be healthy, and not have a serious illness. But when those things happen and we spend years denying the truth, we lose touch with ourselves and our intuition. We start trying to do the impossible and get caught in a downward spiral.

Activity

1 Have you ever faced the loss of something or someone important to you, and then tried to control it? Are you trying to control losing someone or something now? After reading this far, try filling out the blank in this sentence again. I'm powerless over _____ (insert the name of the person or situation you're trying to control)—and my life has become unmanageable.

2 Keep an ongoing list of things, events, and people you can't control. Whenever life starts to feel crazy, ask yourself if you're trying to control someone or something you can't.

Unmanageability

We each have our own unique definition of unmanageability. It can involve neglecting our true responsibilities, denying our emotions, or blaming someone else for our behaviors. Often when a spouse attempts to control a wife or husband, that person begins neglecting the children. The person with the problem becomes the center of the family's attention, and the other family members become neglected.

When our life becomes unmanageable, it's common to feel as though we're crazy. The first time we work Step One, we can feel so crazy and our lives can appear so unmanageable that anyone could see it. But after we've been recovering for a while, we usually set the bar higher for what unmanageability means. As we become healthier, we become more sensitive to the codependent crazies. It may not take long to identify the lack of peace, the angry outburst, the accusations, blaming, denial, arguments, and the rest of the behaviors that accompany alcoholism, addiction, or other compulsive disorders. We can become so healthy that any loss of serenity and peace becomes more than we're willing to accept.

The level of unmanageability that's acceptable depends on our past, how long we've been recovering, and how comfortable we've become with feeling peaceful. One problem with codependency is that it's progressive. Things either get better or worse. Codependency can result in hypochondria, physical or emotional illness, even suicide.

We can begin using alcohol or drugs or engage in other compulsive behavior to medicate emotional pain. We may begin spending money compulsively, either trying to buy good feelings or trying to punish the person responsible for paying the bills. Or we may begin overspending at the therapist's office, expecting him or her to make us better. While therapy can help, our therapist can't do our work. That's up to us.

Admitting we can't control someone or something isn't an excuse to do nothing to solve problems. We take the First Step when we've done all we can reasonably do to solve the problem. Unmanageability sets in when we compulsively do the same things over and over to solve the problem, even though those things don't work. There's a line we cross after we've tried something that doesn't work, but we continue to do it anyway. When we cross that line, we move into the codependency zone. We get stuck like a record or CD, compulsively repeating the same behavior. The more the behavior doesn't work, the harder we try doing it and the crazier we feel. Learn to see the warning signs when that begins to happen. When you feel the codependent crazies, see that yellow light flashing. It means *Alert!* You're reacting codependently. It's time to take the First Step.

Activity

Write about unmanageability and what it means to you. If you're trying to have power where you have none, what are the consequences? Do you feel crazy inside? Write about what that feels like. Have you lost your inner peace? Are you wearing yourself out and annoying other people by doing the same thing over and over, even though what you're doing doesn't work? Keep an ongoing list that describes how unmanageability manifests in your life. Include what it looks like, what it feels like, the behaviors you do, and any people or responsibilities you neglect.

The Power of Detaching

Some spiritual teachers say that we're all connected in ways we can't see and that we're one with everything in the universe, but not in the codependent, overly attached way. We're particularly connected to people we love. We're bonded to them. The First Step can be more difficult the more we love someone. It may feel wrong to let go of someone we care about, or we may think that detaching means we don't love that person. But that isn't what detachment or letting go means. Detachment means we're finally surrendering to the truth. We can't control the other person. Letting go means we acknowledge that we're not responsible for the other person. We're responsible for ourselves.

The First Step is more powerful and potentially healing for everyone than trying to control someone else's behavior. While control is an illusion, surrendering and letting go are real. They're powerful living skills that create healthy and positive consequences instead of unmanageability.

There aren't any guarantees that if we detach and let go, the person we care about will get sober or otherwise do what we want that person to do. But detaching from people we're bonded with can and often does create immediate and visible positive results. Other people can feel it when we stop obsessing and trying to control them. That may be when they finally begin to see themselves. Up until then, they may have been so busy reacting to our attempts to control them that they lost sight of what they were doing and how they were hurting themselves. When we stop obsessing, they feel the release.

It's like cutting the string on a helium balloon. It flies up into the air. We've set it free. It can go anywhere the wind blows it. When we let go of someone we're close to and set them free, they may become frightened. They don't like being on their own. Playing the game of reacting to us distracted them from what they were doing and gave them a reason to blame us. Now they have to face themselves. Ironically, when we finally cut them loose, it's not unusual for people to decide of their own free will to do what we've spent so much time trying to force them to do.

In a dating situation, where we've been obsessing about the other person—will he or she call, does he or she care about me—our obsessive behavior can drive the other person away. When we stop obsessing and learn to be present for ourselves, the other person, and each moment, we're learning what it really means to love. When we let go, that person may begin pursuing us because we're no longer chasing them away with our obsessing and controlling gestures.

Letting go with love and detachment begin transformation. The first behavior gives the other person to God's care. The second behavior means we don't engage with craziness by interacting with someone's disease through arguing, denying, or engaging in any behavior that is nonproductive, doesn't work, and wastes energy.

Even if the other person doesn't change, we'll change by practicing these new behaviors. Whatever we're trying to control is really controlling us. We are the person we set free when we work Step One.

When we're busy trying to control someone or something, we don't relax and we're not present for life. Sometimes we discover that we don't even want whatever it is we've been so ferociously obsessing about and trying to make happen! We began obsessing, and then it became a habit.

Congratulations. You're on your way to the top of the mountain and a new life.

Activity

Keep a record of the changes and consequences that occur in situations when you let go. The next time you get hooked into a situation and begin trying to control it, read your list. See for yourself the good things that happen from *Letting go and letting God* and detaching with love. Sometimes we've been involved with an insane situation for so long that we can't detach with love initially. All we feel is anger. It's okay to start there, but detaching with love and with respect for the other person should be our ultimate goal.

Apply Step One as Needed

We can use Step One in many situations other than those involving alcoholism and addictions. Often when a writer or artist faces a creative project, the first approach is to try to control it. The harder the person tries to control it, the more unmanageable the project becomes. It's another place we can use the First Step. This can happen when we try to fix anything that's broken, or do something we haven't yet learned to do.

Alcoholics, addicts, and people with other compulsive behaviors can use this Step to avoid relapsing in their addiction. "I'd been sober about a year when my mind went blank," said someone who now has eighteen years of sober living by working the Steps. "I watched a lot of people who went to treatment start drinking or using drugs again. One night I couldn't see any reason I shouldn't start using again too. I'd been working so hard on my sobriety and doing the right things. Why should everyone else have the fun and take the easy route while I did all the hard work? I called my sponsor to talk to him about how I felt and the crazy way I was thinking. I couldn't find him. I didn't know what to do. I was about an hour away from that first drink, which for alcoholics can be the start of the end of recovery. I sat in my apartment and asked, *Why shouldn't I have a drink?* I couldn't think of an answer. Finally, I heard it: *I'm powerless over alcohol and my life has become unmanageable.* That's why I shouldn't drink. When I do, my life becomes insane. I chose not to drink because I didn't want the consequences: a life that's unmanageable."

We can work Step One when a feeling such as anger overwhelms us, and we can't get past it. The unmanageability from too much anger may cause us to be resentful and bitter. That is when it is time to apply Step One: *I'm powerless over my anger, and my life has become unmanageable.*

Step One can be applied to financial problems. Maybe we're overspending. Or maybe we've been hit with a severe financial crisis, something we can't control. We become frightened. We panic. What's going to happen? We stop living in the present moment and get tangled up in the what ifs of the future. We can do this so long and hard that we become an emotional wreck. Apply the First Step. *I'm powerless over finances, and my life has become unmanageable.*

Some people lose control with eating. *I'm powerless over food.*

Some get caught up in fear and panic. For no observable cause, a person may have a panic attack. The fear is overwhelming. "I go fetal, literally," said one man. "I crawl into bed, get under the covers, and get all balled up like a fetus in the womb." Many people who identify as codependents have a lot of anxiety and fear. It may legitimately be the emotions of anxiety and fear that they feel. Or it could be a mishmash of many repressed emotions from their past. When these emotions come up, they can feel similar to a panic attack. *I'm powerless over my fear and anxiety, and my life has become unmanageable.* Or, if you think it's a group of repressed emotions from the past: *I'm powerless over old, repressed emotions, and my life has become unmanageable.*

Become familiar with the First Step. Sometimes all we have to do is think about a Step, and that's enough to work it. Let it take you smoothly through any situation that otherwise could become rocky. Phobias are another area where working the First Step is an appropriate action. Agoraphobia is when a person becomes afraid to leave his or her house. People with this phobia can't give you a logical reason why they're afraid to leave their homes, but they cannot open the door and go where they want to go. The phobia has trapped them inside their homes; their homes become prisons. The First Step can be applied here or to other phobias. *I'm powerless over my fear of leaving my home, and my life has become unmanageable.*

The First Step doesn't mean we aren't responsible for our behaviors. By taking the First Step, we're given the ability to take appropriate and responsible actions. We may learn to apply Step One in record time, with enough practice, in many situations. It'll be like someone inserted new software programming in our minds. We'll scan the situation and try to solve the problem legitimately. You may want to try a problem-solving action up to three times, but usually three times is the limit for trying a particular solution. When you've done everything you can plus a little more, it's time to *Let go and let God.* Maybe we'll have the power to do something at another time. Maybe not. The problem might work itself out. The future isn't ours to control. Let life take its course.

Activity

1 From today forward, when you encounter a problem with a person or situation that engages you, tempting you to try to control it, review the situation before taking any action. Decide what healthy, normal problem-solving skills you can use in the situation. Attempt to come up with at least three reasonable solutions. Then keep track of how many times you apply each solution to the problem. Note when you've tried a solution three times and it hasn't worked. It doesn't mean the problem will never be solved or that you can't solve it later. But it's clear that you can't solve it now. Learning to effectively evaluate situations and keeping track of our attempts to solve problems can help us become more skilled at both solving problems and learning to let go. Remember, detaching is an action too.

2 If you're already in a Twelve Step program, what did you admit powerlessness over originally, and how did your life become unmanageable? Write about it so if you ever hit a blank spot and can't see any good reason why you shouldn't start doing the behavior again, you can read your story and remember why you shouldn't drink, use drugs, or do whatever you did that created unmanageability in your life in the first place.

Whether we're beginning the journey of recovery from codependency or we're solving another problem, taking the First Step isn't just a good way to begin. It's the only way. It's normal to feel hopeless, depressed, sad, or any number of emotions when we take this Step and realize we've been trying to do the impossible—and in so doing, we made a mess. It can also bring up feelings of sadness if it involves acknowledging the possibility of an important loss.

Emotions, like anything else, come to pass. The good news is that the First Step in recovering from codependency begins a journey of healing for us. The other good news is that it's not a one-Step program. We won't be entrenched in Step One and any feelings of despondency for the rest of our lives.

In His great wisdom, the Creator gave us a way to climb higher and get out of any despair and hopelessness that come from admitting and accepting powerlessness. If taking the First Step has you feeling blue, you don't have to stay there. Turn the page and work Step Two.

The Believers

"It has also been my experience that

my Higher Power seems reluctant to intervene

in my circumstances until I accept what

He has already given me."

—Codependent No More

Suggested reading: chapter 12, "Learn the Art of Acceptance"

STEP TWO: Came to believe that a Power greater than ourselves could restore us to sanity.

—from the TWELVE STEPS OF CO-DEPENDENTS ANONYMOUS

For some people, this is the easiest of all the Steps. But it's essential, so it's important not to skip it, the way we sometimes take two steps at once on a stairway. If we're sincere in our desire to work this program, life will bring us what we need to work this Step in a way that's right for each of us.

See!

Many people are amazed when they first see people living peacefully, not trying to control and not being controlled by situations similar to theirs. When we see that someone else felt the way we feel, and then transcended those feelings and became transformed by working these Steps, we believe the Twelve Steps just might work for us too.

This is true whether we're trying to stop using drugs, stop controlling an alcoholic, or stop being controlled by our fears.

Going to Twelve Step meetings, listening to other people's stories, and reading books is important. These actions expose us to someone who's done the work. It's what keeps Twelve Step groups going and growing. We're exposed to someone who's been transformed by working the Steps. We believe that transformation can happen to us, so we work the Steps and become transformed too. Then newcomers come to the meetings and see us. They come to believe the Steps and this program can work for them. The torch is carried from one person and handed to the next. The light continues to burn.

People say the past can't be changed, but that's not true. This program can take the worst things we've done and recycle them into healing for others. Life uses what we've done to help other people believe that they can successfully begin this new way of life, and that these Steps will work for them. No matter what we've done or been through, life can use our worst experiences to benefit others.

Seeing how our mistakes can help others heal creates good feelings. It leads to self-forgiveness and higher self-esteem.

Have you come to believe that God as you understand God can restore you and your life to sanity, bring peace where there's been chaos, love where there's been hatred, and faith where there's been fear? Have you come to believe you can let go of the other person and take care of yourself? Have you come to believe it's safe to stop controlling?

Groups become stale and membership dwindles when the people attending don't work the Steps. Newcomers don't see anyone changing. They don't see anything in anyone that they want to have. All they hear is griping and complaining. Most of us can do that on our own, all by ourselves. Newcomers to those kinds of groups don't come to believe. Instead they come, and then they leave without ever believing that they'll change and that recovery will work for them. We can either become a role model and a healing force in the community, or we can be one more person who chooses to stay a victim. Climbing the mountain isn't easy. Neither is living a miserable life. Are you willing to become a believer?

> **"I saw a group of people at Al-Anon who lived with situations similar to mine, where someone they loved wouldn't stop drinking and it tore them apart. Yet these people smiled at me, and their smiles were genuine. I couldn't remember the last time I smiled. They reflected inner peace, but chaos filled my soul. I wanted the same light in my eyes that shined in theirs. I kept going to meetings because I wanted what they found."**
>
> —Annie M.

"I started writing in a journal every day after I began attending Co-Dependents Anonymous meetings. By documenting how I felt and the changes in and around me, I saw something I liked—the way that my relationships were being transformed."

———·•·———

—*Taylor S.*

"I watched one of the craziest people I know turn into a sane, respectable, and responsible person. This woman had truly been psychotic. I knew if she could change, I could too. Ever since, I've attended meetings."

———·•·———

—*Mike T.*

Many different events can help us come to believe that change is possible for us. Hope replaces despair. We see change in others or we begin to see it in ourselves. Some people say that faith means we believe first, and then we can see. But when it comes to changing behaviors that have been lifetime survival behaviors, we often need to see first, before we can believe that change is possible for us.

Activity

1. Have you formally worked Step Two yet? If you're on this lesson, it means you admitted there's been some insanity and unmanageability in your life. Do you believe you can be restored to peace and sanity? How did you come to believe that? Do you remember a specific instance and time when that belief occurred? Write about it. It's an important lesson to document.

2. If you're attending groups and someone asks you to lead a meeting or share your story, do it. Your experience could be exactly what someone else needs to hear. If you're not going to groups or meetings but you're still working on changing your codependent behaviors, be honest and open with people who still suffer from codependency. It's not your business to tell anyone what to do, but you can talk about what you're doing. Don't pretend to be perfect. Be honest about who you are. Tell the truth about what your life was like, what happened, and what your life is like now. Being honest about ourselves—who we are and how we're being transformed—takes courage, but it's an act of love that can bring others hope and healing. Your story is important. Share it whenever you can.

This Higher Power Thing

Some people resist the Higher Power part of Twelve Step programs. But some Steps, including this one, specifically mention God and the words *Higher Power.* They also give ample room for individual belief systems by saying, "God as we understand God."

In the beginning of the recovery revolution, people said things such as, "Anything, including a doorknob, can be your Higher Power." A personal relationship with a doorknob wouldn't change me much. I can't see myself asking a doorknob for help. The idea was that we're supposed to stop playing God and understand that there's a Power greater than us, and not let any negative past ideas or understanding of God or religion hinder our progress.

Twelve Step groups are more than self-help programs. They're a spiritual recovery process. I haven't seen one person change significantly without working a spiritual program. A big part of codependency is having an unrealistic relationship with power. Codependents believe they have more power than they do. They often think it's their job to change and control other people. It's important that people healing from codependency issues know that there's a Power greater than ourselves, and we don't have to do His job.

Due to the pain and abuse many people recovering from codependency have endured, they've either lost faith in God or believe that God doesn't care about them. *If He did, why would He let this happen?* But Twelve Step groups aren't religious groups. They're spiritual, and there's a difference. Part of recovery includes discovering that difference for ourselves.

The primary purpose for each specific group is spelled out in that group's traditions. For instance, the primary purpose of Al-Anon and Alateen is to "help families and friends of alcoholics recover from the effects of living with the problem drinking of a relative or friend, whether the alcoholic recovers or not." The primary purpose of Co-Dependents Anonymous, according to the bylaws of Co-Dependents Anonymous, Inc., is to "carry its message to Co-Dependents who still suffer."

The list goes on for each meeting or group for particular types of codependency, but never is the primary purpose to convert a member or potential member to any religion. Affiliation with politics, religions, or denominations is prohibited in all the groups' traditions. On our own time, we're each free to be involved with whatever religion we choose.

Our job in recovery is to grow in our relationship and understanding of God as we each understand Him. We truly begin to grow when our understanding of our Higher Power turns into a personal relationship with Him, when we know that God is real, and when we feel that He knows and cares about each of us.

Some women who have been abused by their fathers have expressed difficulty turning their wills and lives over to the care of an omnipotent God referred to as a *male father figure*. That's understandable. To them, a father represents control, abuse, manipulation, and fear. That's why we have the freedom to understand God for ourselves, and why it's crucial not to impose our beliefs on anyone else or let anyone impose his or her beliefs on us.

It's not my job to tell you how to understand your Higher Power. The Steps suggest that we each come to some understanding of God. I've yet to hear anyone clearly and concisely explain how, exactly, he or she understands God. Most people at meetings will vigorously tell you what they believe God isn't. The God of recovery isn't a God of abuse or revenge. He's not one who punishes. He loves and forgives us, and hears us whenever we sincerely talk to Him.

That's good enough for me.

Activity

Track your understanding of a Higher Power. Write about how you understood God as a child and, if that understanding has changed, how you understand God now. Also keep track of any spiritual experiences or awakenings you've had. Keep an ongoing log that reflects your experiences as you grow in your understanding of what a Higher Power means to you, how you connect with God, and how God connects with you.

What Do You See?

Off and on over the past hundred years, people have written and continue to write about the power of goal setting. That includes visualizing—seeing in our mind what we want to happen. In 1978, Shakti Gawain released her book *Creative Visualization: Use the Power of Your Imagination to Create What You Want in Your Life.* Sports leaders have honed their skills by practicing their particular sport in their mind's eye for many years.

Although the Second Step says to pray only for knowledge of God's will for us and the power to carry it out, it's important to set goals too. It's equally important to let go of our goals and let God work things out in our lives.

"What I regret most about my recovery from codependency is that I didn't include setting goals for myself, goals that included using my creativity, creating my dreams, and doing meaningful work," one anonymous recovering woman said.

Many of us believe we don't deserve to have and achieve our dreams, and that's sad. It's easy to keep the bar set low for ourselves in all parts of our life: work, relationships, money.

But this Step conveys two important ideas if we read them carefully. One is that we don't do the changing ourselves. A Power greater than ourselves—most likely not a doorknob—changes us if we do our part and work the Steps. The other important idea Step Two tells us is that our part is believing.

If we're going to believe, why not set the bar higher?

I believe in setting goals, and then letting them go. I believe we should be as specific as possible about what we want to happen. "Be careful of asking for what you want. You might get it," some naysayers warn. I believe that's an ominous, negative response to what we desire and want.

While I don't advocate self-will or seeking fame and fortune, I urge you to use goal setting and creative visualization along with Step Two to create a rich, full life for yourself. The athletes who use visualization as part of training agree that there's little difference between seeing something in our mind and actually having the experience. Test this theory. Imagine how you'd feel if someone you trusted told you that something dreadful happened, and you believed that person. You'd feel exactly the same as you would if it actually happened.

One night when I first began setting goals, I wrote down all my hopes and dreams. When I finished, the thought occurred to me: *If you could have anything you wanted and it wouldn't be bad or wrong, what would that be?* So I added that, and put everything I wanted on my goal list. Although it might take five, ten, or thirty-five years for some goals to manifest, every goal I wrote on that piece of paper turned into reality. I didn't have to make things happen. I became clear about what I wanted, and I became willing to pay my dues. Then I turned my goal list and my desires over to my Higher Power, ending my goal sheet with the words *Thy will be done.*

Then I continued to show up for life *One day at a time.*

If you're going to go for your dreams, go big. But also go with an equally large amount of humility. Plant the seeds for your dreams by setting and visualizing your goals. Then *Let go and let God* do the growing.

In recovery it's called *Fake it until we make it*, or *Acting as if.*

Activity

1. Set written goals. Spend time visualizing what you want your life to look like. Be specific. Include how you want your life to feel, what you see yourself doing, and how you imagine you will feel. Write as many goals as you want. If you don't know what you want, make discovering that your first goal. Then let go, get up every day, and live your life.

2. Add new items to your goal list every six months. Set new goals when you get stuck, when your life becomes stagnant, when you

Activity (cont.)

don't know what to do or where to go next, when you reach your current goals, and when you don't feel as though you have a life or ever will. If you could have, do, and be whatever you wanted, what would that be? Be clear about why you want your goals—your motivation and agenda. Tip: The more your goals involve service, the more likely it is that your dreams will come true.

③ If the thought of setting goals intimidates you, go to the library or bookstore and get some books on goal setting and creative visualization. Then read the books. Practice what they suggest. Like anything else, the theories in the books won't work unless you work them.

Use the Tools in Your Kit

Recovery offers us many tools to aid in our spiritual growth. At the "Addictionz" Web site, www.addictionz.com, Dean Brandhagen gathered the most all-inclusive, comprehensive collection of Twelve Step sayings, slogans, and proverbs that I've ever seen, heard, or read. These sayings and slogans have a long shelf life. They've been around for a long time. The reason for that is that they work. They help us come to believe, especially those days when we aren't certain if there's any hope for us.

Sayings like the ones I use in this book have power because they're simple to follow and they're true. *Act as if* means that even if we don't believe something or feel a certain way, we can *Fake it until we make it*. We've used denial for so many years in a negative way. *Fake it until we make it* means that we can use the positive side of denial by pretending we can succeed until we do. We force ourselves to think and feel as though we're already who we want to become.

One more slogan that's important is *Progress not perfection*. We don't have to work any Step perfectly. All we need to do at any moment is the best that we can.

Activity

1. Become familiar with program sayings and slogans. One source for these slogans is Dean Brandhagen's "Addictionz" Web site. If you stop by his site, be sure to thank him. Copy your favorite sayings on small pieces of paper. Then put them somewhere where you'll see them often. Choose the ones that speak to you. Another saying is *Take what you like and leave the rest*. Use whatever you need from the recovery program to get through each day peacefully, with love for yourself and others. If something doesn't help you, don't talk badly about it. It might help someone else, or it may be what you need on another day.

2. In Lesson One, I wrote a list of affirmations to assist you in changing. Now I'm handing the power to you. Write out and read daily the affirmations you need to help you *Come to believe that a Power greater than yourself can restore you to sanity* or that He already is doing that. Work this Step until you know that change can be as real for you as it is for anyone else—if you do your work.

Using This Step in Daily Life

Step Two is crucial the first time we work the Steps the thorough way, when we begin the process of consciously growing and changing. But almost all of the Steps make handy little daily tools. That includes this one.

When we become aware of a problem we can't solve, or we'd like to whip through the solution a little faster, we can apply Step One by thinking to ourselves that we're powerless over whatever it is that we can't change. Then we move right up through as many Steps as we need to in order to fix the problem.

Step Two, coming to believe that a Power greater than ourselves could restore us to sanity, is useful whenever we start controlling, caretaking, or repeatedly trying to do something that doesn't work. Often all we have to do is think this Step, and that's enough to do the trick.

We can get to a place in our recovery where we zip through these Steps whenever we get stuck, don't know what to do, or need help setting a boundary. It takes the power and pressure off us. We acknowledge we don't have to change ourselves because God changes us.

It's easy to get caught up in the "self-help" or "do-it-yourself" way of thinking, especially for codependents. Many of us have felt alone and separated from everything and everyone for much of our lives. If anything needed doing, we had to do it ourselves. That doesn't apply to spiritual growth and change. We need to do our part. We need to work the best program that we can. But we don't have to transform ourselves.

That's God's job.

Take a deep breath. Look around. You have a right to be here. You matter and you count. Where you are is where you belong. This world that may have been so unkind transforms as we transform. What you believe is what you'll get.

Activity

1. Become aware of what a helpful tool Step Two is. Watch for situations in your daily life where you can use Steps One and Two together to help you solve annoying problems. Often smaller problems can be as aggravating as the big ones.

2. If you're having trouble with the Higher Power part of this program, write a letter to God. Ask Him to show you in a way you can understand that He cares about you and your spiritual growth. Tell Him you need to feel His touch to help you believe He cares. Then watch for the answer, because it will come.

I'm not going to tell you to do something you want to do before you move on to the next lesson. You decide when it's time to move on to Lesson Four. You decide if you feel like treating yourself, or if you need a rest or break. Making decisions about how to take care of yourself and what you need is your job, and part of working a good program.

These are real powers you possess.

Surrender to Destiny

". . . forcing my will on any given situation

eliminates the possibility of my Higher Power

doing anything constructive about that situation,

the person, or me."

—Codependent No More

Suggested reading: chapter 7, "Set Yourself Free"

STEP THREE: Made a decision to turn our will and our lives over to the care of God as we understood God.

—*from the* TWELVE STEPS OF CO-DEPENDENTS ANONYMOUS

As you're beginning to see, especially if this is your first exposure to the Twelve Steps and what it means to work them, the action we're to take is clearly spelled out in the first part of each Step. In Step One, we admit that we're powerless over something or someone, and the result of us trying to have power where we have none is unmanageability or, as related to the Second Step, a lifestyle that's less than sane. If we back off and look at it, in time we'll grow to recognize the action called for in the First Step as surrender to reality, the truth, and the loss we've been trying to prevent.

The Second Step calls for a slightly less clear action: *We came to believe that a Power greater than ourselves could restore us to sanity.* It could mean we grow into believing that we can be restored to sanity and our lives can be restored to being manageable. By whatever method or action, we begin to think and believe a new way about ourselves, God, and our lives. This Step relieves us of the burden of having to change ourselves, or pull ourselves up by our bootstraps, or use willpower to change. It tells us that a Power greater than ourselves will transform us.

Choosing the Designer for Your Life's Plan and Purpose

Step Three asks us to step up to the plate and make a decision. It's an intense choice, and brings deeper implications than, for instance, deciding what kind of cereal or peanut butter we're going to buy at the grocery store. We're choosing to turn the steering wheel of our lives over to God. Although we're given ample room for how we define God, this Step clearly states that it's a spiritual power that we're giving the reins to, not a lamppost, a doorknob, or a jelly jar.

We're choosing to let our Higher Power direct the course of our lives, to go along with the Divine Plan for our lives, and to give to God that invisible but important powerhouse of ambition and fuel that we call our *will*. We're forfeiting self-will, but that doesn't mean we're becoming doormats or limp shells of our past selves. We're aligning that part of ourselves that drives us forward with God's will and plan for us. This Step implies that there is a plan, that we each have a divine destiny and there's a reason we're here on earth.

In this Step, we're making a commitment to forgo self-will and surrender to God's plan. We're going to let Him guide us, and we'll turn our will over to Him.

For anyone used to micromanaging things and controlling people, this new way of living can challenge our core beliefs about what we need to do to feel safe and secure. Exciting? Not at first. It feels more frightening than walking a tightrope blindfolded. Gradually, as we relax into God's arms and let go a little, we see that living this way makes for a much more interesting journey through the world. We can't figure things out, and we don't have to. We aren't certain what will happen next. Often, although we know we're in the midst of a lesson, we can't see (because we aren't supposed to) exactly what it is that we're trying to learn. If we knew, we'd mess with the educational process. Life is becoming experiential. Soon it's going to become an adventure. That's when it's a fun way to live.

"My mother sent me to church on Sundays and church camp during the summer," one Double Winner said. "I took it for granted that there's a God. But by the time I became a teenager, I'd lived with so much abuse, abandonment, and emotional pain that I became fed up with and angry at God. I made a clear decision one day to take my will back and do it myself.

"I was on my way to church and almost there when suddenly I said, 'Whoa. Wait a minute.' I stopped to think this through. People have plastered signs on the walls at church that read *God is love*. But not much of what's happened to me even remotely resembles love. If it does, I don't want it. God can give that kind of love to someone else. I looked up at the sky. 'I'll take it from here, thank you anyway,' I said. Then I did the exact opposite of what this Step says. I took my life and will back from God's care. I didn't think I could do a better job than God had, but I figured I couldn't do much worse.

"I was wrong. The path I chose led me to becoming a strung-out junkie with an arrest record as long as my needle-tracked arms by the time I hit my early twenties. When I reached the Third Step, I'd already started crying 'Uncle' from all the pain inside. I'd become totally ready to surrender to whatever God had in store. Finally, I'd run out of myself and my will. If He wanted me, He could have me. Nobody else wanted anything to do with me—including myself. Running the show and functioning on self-will had driven me into the ground. I was more than ready to take the Third Step, so I did. Life continued to be what it is with extreme highs and lows. But from the day I first worked the Third Step in Alcoholics Anonymous and later followed that by working it again in Al-Anon, I learned that no matter what mountains appeared in my path, a way would be made for me to go over, through, or around them, and usually, I'd climb to the top. For whatever problems I had, the solutions I needed also appeared. The good part and the God part was that I could find this way without drinking or using drugs. But it took me more than a decade to get these lessons under my belt. I didn't understand much while the learning process was going on.

"Years later, I became suicidal from my codependent behaviors and the consequences they created. Controlling, taking care of others, suppressing what I felt, obsessing about other people, and neglecting myself drove me into the ground again. I made the decision to turn my will and my life over to the care of God again, this time in a different Twelve Step program.

"In AA, working the Third Step meant I'd be shown a way to get through whatever happened without using drugs. In Al-Anon, it meant so much more. It gave me permission to be good to myself. Alcoholics Anonymous taught us we shouldn't say no whenever somebody in the program asked us for help. Al-Anon not only gave me permission to say no, but the program finally taught me how and gave me the power to do it.

"Al-Anon isn't an easier, softer way, the kind the Big Book of Alcoholics Anonymous warns about. But it does involve a more self-loving way of living. I began to practice behaviors that helped me recover from codependency: feeling my emotions, speaking up for myself, setting boundaries and limits, and then enforcing them. The way or path through whatever happened expanded. Now I had room to feel emotions, including anger. While Alcoholics Anonymous cautioned us about feeling that emotion, codependency recovery encouraged it.

"Here's another example of the differences in the Twelve Step programs. In AA, I interpreted God's will for me to mean that I always took care of other people and forgot about what I needed and wanted. AA looked at self-will with disdain and disapproval. Al-Anon taught me that it was essential to trust myself. I learned that if something felt right to me, I could trust my impressions. Usually what felt right and good to me would be God's plans for me, not some disobedient flurry of self-will run riot and acting out. What I had a passion to do would be my higher purpose. I wouldn't be stuck trudging through some dreary life plan I found boring and repulsive. If I did my work, then my dreams, wishes, desires, and goals would be aligned with God's purpose. I'd be one with my Higher Power. No more battling over wills.

"Once I redefined what turning my life and will over to God's care really means, I realized I could trust what I wanted to do. If I actively worked the Steps, if I daily asked God for direction and guidance, I could then trust what felt right and good to me instead of thinking that anything that felt good to me was an inappropriate display of self-will.

"It's not that AA disrespects people, or holds them and their desires in contempt. I'm not blaming the AA program. My codependency issues caused my confusion. They created my misinterpretation of the Steps. I didn't like myself, didn't trust myself, couldn't feel my feelings, and saw anything I wanted as bad and wrong, until I began to treat myself with love and respect. When I addressed my codependency, God's will expanded. I could break the dysfunctional codependency rules that say you can't think, can't feel, can't take care of yourself, and can't have fun. This divine will finally opened the gates to a rich and loving life, the one I'd been searching for all along.

"The AA program taught me that God is real. Codependency recovery taught me that I'm real and that I deserve to be loved. I can fully express the person I am.

"Throughout my life, I'd turned my life and will over to various uncaring men. That became a disaster. Then I turned my life over to the care of alcohol and drugs. That didn't work well, either. It became brutal when I turned my will over to the care of a practicing alcoholic when I was in recovery for chemical dependency myself. What a mess! I spent most of my time wishing that one of us—either my husband or myself—would die. Sometimes I even counted the days until I thought that might happen. In retrospect, I see that I was doing what trapped people do—fighting for my freedom. I just didn't know how to go about it yet. But when I finally began working two programs, one for my chemical dependency and one for my codependency, that became the winning combination. Pieces weren't missing anymore. I had God, myself, and the two programs I needed. That's when life and recovery began to make sense."

Activity

1. Who's creating the plan for your life? Did you have an incident that stands out where you took your life back from a Higher Power? Before being exposed to the Third Step, did you think about who had control of your life and will? Did you have or are you willing to have an experience where you give control of your life to God, either again or for the first time?

2. What do the terms *surrendering to God's will, Divine Plan,* and *destiny* mean to you?

3. Do you believe you have a destiny and it's safe for you to surrender to it? Are you confident you'll find it by surrendering to God's will? Do you believe you can trust yourself, that the desires of your heart are aligned with your true spiritual purpose, and will get you where God wants you to go? Or do you believe that

Activity (cont.)

Activity (cont.)

whatever you want is bad and wrong—that God's will is strict, harsh, or severe? Is there room in God's will for you to love yourself? Write about God's will for your life and what you think that involves. If you have any fears, write about them too. Do you believe your destiny is to take care of other people? Do you believe someone should take care of you because you take care of him or her? Or do you know that you can gently, lovingly, but with discipline when necessary, take care of yourself?

Level of Commitment

Mountain climbers use a term called *level of commitment*. True mountain climbing, not the step climbing I did in China, can be challenging and dangerous. It involves using all the tools available to find a path, sometimes scaling a mountainside that's straight up and down. Sometimes people climbing a mountain don't know much about the rest of the climb, how hard or easy it'll be, but usually they have the experiences of others who have climbed before them to draw on, and those experiences help them.

Serious mountain climbers consider the challenges before they climb. They study the path, what others have encountered, and then, especially when they're climbing with a group or another person, they state their level of commitment. When the going gets rough, if it should become dangerous, or if the weather gets severe, will they continue? Unless it becomes foolhardy and self-destructive, will they continue climbing? What will it take to make them stop the climb?

People put much preparation and money into climbs. They want to know that the other people in their group are at the same level of commitment that they're at. On a scale of one to ten, with one being the least committed, how committed are they to completing the climb? Will they quit at the first sign of discomfort or problems—give up and go home? Or are they at a ten? Short of an avalanche or serious injury that prevents them from safely going forward, or weather conditions that make it unadvisable to continue, are they fully committed to the climb?

Over the years, I've known people in all different types of recovery programs, and I've seen different levels of commitment. "I'll stay sober as long as it doesn't hurt too much." "I'll continue taking care of myself as long as nobody challenges me, or I don't face losing someone or something important."

I can almost promise that life will test you on your level of commitment. You will come face to face with that one thing that could cause you to take back your decision to turn your will and life over to God's care.

Know where you stand. Be prepared in advance. We work this program a day at a time. We can only be in the moment, and live today. But we can prepare for tomorrow proactively by knowing where we stand and how committed to recovery we are. When the test comes, which it will, we'll have our decision to fall back on. We'll know how committed we are to the climb.

Activity

1. On a scale of one to ten, rate your level of commitment to healing from your codependency issues. Are you in it for the long haul, no matter what?

2. Have you put any conditions on your decision to turn your life and will over to God's care? We each have a good idea if we have conditions and what these conditions are. What are yours? What's the thing or event that would stop you from recovering and taking care of yourself, the condition you've put on your journey into self-love?

3. Are you willing to make an unconditional commitment to recovery and to taking good, healthy care of yourself? Are you willing to make a commitment to staying with yourself and the process through all kinds of emotions and distress, through the hard work and the good days, and take your recovery all the way? Are you willing to let go of your victim self-image? Are you willing to back off from giving until you've learned how to give in healthy ways? Are you willing to continue taking care of yourself, making decisions that reflect self-love and respect, even if that means you don't get married or have children? Are you willing to stay with recovery even if that means you don't achieve fortune or fame, and your destiny is to work a humble job that serves other people in another way, maybe not as grandiose as you'd prefer?

A Daily Choice

I love it when I hear people talk about spending a few extra seconds in bed each morning, or beginning their day by getting on their knees and praying so they can daily turn their life and will over to the care of God. It's an excellent way to begin any day. When I start the day with my Higher Power, things go better. I'm more prepared to handle whatever comes my way.

Simple rituals can help us remember the new way of life we're striving to live. How could there be a better way to start each day than with a conscious choice to turn our life and will over to God?

Activity

Come up with a ritual that will help you renew your decision to work the Third Step each day. It can be as part of a morning prayer or meditation, or simply taking the time to renew your commitment by reading Step Three. Whether you've been working a Twelve Step program for twenty years or two days, this is a good habit to develop and a tremendous way to start each day.

The Trio

Many people in recovery group Steps One, Two, and Three together. These three Steps work great as daily problem-solving tools. We encounter a person, problem, or situation. It doesn't matter how big or little. What matters is that it's more powerful than we are, and it's taking over our lives.

When that something happens, we admit we can't control it and that things get crazy when and if we try. We recall that there's a Power greater than ourselves who knows our name and cares enough about us to reach down and help us. Then we acknowledge that there's a loving path through whatever this problem is, and we surrender to God's plan and will for us. Then we trust that where we're going isn't an accident or a mistake. It's the perfect destiny for us.

After years of practice, we can become so skilled at applying this trio to any situation we can't control that it becomes a habitual reaction. We can get so good at this that we can apply Steps One through Three in the right order in five minutes or less. It's a winning behavior trio that helps us think straight and smoothly move through whatever life sends to us.

You'll be surprised at how effective these three Steps can be as a first-line approach to whatever life throws our way.

But how do I know if what I'm doing is my will or God's will for me? How do I know the difference between self-will and divine will?

Hush. Don't worry about that now. The answers to those questions will come later, with another Step. Work on developing a realistic relationship with control and power, admit when you're tangling with someone or something more powerful than you, and remember that you don't have to pull yourself up by your own bootstraps. Let go. Acknowledge that God cares, that you need to do your part in taking care of yourself, and then give God control over your life.

First things first. Before you decide what you're going to do, choose who the director of your life will be. God or you? The details will come after that.

Activity

Keep a record of when you use this trio. Include the first time, when your approach to these Steps is thorough, and then include the other situations when you apply the trio to the daily problems. Soon you'll see that using these Steps keeps you in that remarkable place that's the opposite of insanity and unmanageability. It's called *grace*.

Who's Your Daddy, and Do You Trust Him?

Before we end this lesson, another aspect of this Step needs to be stressed. It's going to be difficult, if not impossible, to turn our will and lives over to the care of anything or anyone unless we trust what is controlling and caring for our life. This Step calls for a big leap of faith.

Many of us have endured abuse of all kinds. We may have been lied to and betrayed, or had to surrender to cruel and inhuman treatment of all kinds. How can we trust a Higher Power who let those events occur?

The answer is simple but not easy: We make a decision to trust our Higher Power one day at a time.

Life is going to be life. It will do what it does. Look back at history and the stories of people on a spiritual quest. Not many have had it easy. Not many people seem to be given everything they wanted without big losses, disappointments, or betrayals.

I can recall the first time in recovery when life threw a nasty, ugly problem my way. I went to my counselor, complaining about my difficulty. My counselor responded with that classic answer, "Nobody ever said it was going to be easy."

That may be true, but nobody ever told me it was going to be as hard as it's been. For a long time, I felt tricked and betrayed. You may not have to go through any hard, horrible experiences. But then again, you may have to endure more pain than you thought you could.

When my son died, I became furious with God and life. It doesn't get much more painful than that. Or it might. All my children could have died, and I could have lost both legs. Usually, when bad things happen, it could have been worse. But that doesn't do much to help our pain.

I've been incredibly blessed in recovery, and at times I've been painfully cursed. My first fifteen years, I lived in poverty. After my son died, I cried every day for the next eight years. I've seen wonderful things happen to people, as well as terrible tragedies. There are no guarantees, but chances are that at some point, life is going to hurt like hell. That person or thing you valued most may be what you're going to lose. You may have to live without the one thing you said you couldn't or wouldn't. The blessings are going to be better than you can imagine, but you may also go through pain that's so intense you think it couldn't get any worse.

That's the truth about the spiritual path. Go in, eyes wide open. Don't worry about what will occur and when. The things we worry about aren't usually the ones that happen. The things that cause the most pain will catch us by surprise some ordinary Saturday afternoon, and life will never again be the same. Or the phone will ring in the middle of the night with news that changes your life. Or just when you think life couldn't get any better, you'll be blindsided and you won't have any control. To make it worse, people may not be compassionate. They may think it's your fault even though it's not. If they think it happened to you because you did something wrong, then they'll think they're safe and it won't happen to them. Few people are skilled at being truly compassionate and comforting of people in grief. You may have to learn to comfort yourself.

That's when you'll learn the real meaning of *doing your own work.*

I hope you're the exception. But if that difficult and painful thing happens, remember that somebody warned you that it might. Do you have the chutzpah to go about your daily business, turning your life and will over to the care of your Higher Power, knowing that God is real, and so omnipotent and all-powerful He could have prevented it from happening, but didn't? That you can still trust Him anyway, because by now you know that's the only way you'll get through?

Good. I'm glad we got that out of the way.

Make every moment count. None of us knows how much time we have left or what lies ahead. But we can't live our lives worrying about who might die or what tragedies might happen. That's no way to live. Be present each moment for yourself and the people you love. Grace is like breathing. We can't get ahead of ourselves; we only get the breath we need now, and we only get one breath at a time. We won't get grace to go through problems that haven't happened, but we'll get it when and if they occur.

Let go and let God take you through your destiny. Know you're loved, and that no matter what happens to you, you're not alone. It's happened to other people too.

The grass isn't greener on the right side, the left side, ahead of us, or behind us. And so what if it is? You've got to tend to your own matters. When good things happen to someone else, they didn't get your stuff. Don't waste your time envying or resenting them. Unless you broke a law and you're getting a legitimate legal consequence, know that if something bad happens, you're not being singled out or punished for anything you've done.

When you get to the top of that mountain and then down the other side, the next one will appear on your path. When you master one lesson, the next course will begin, and sometimes it will start before you've had time to catch your breath. That's the way life is. We go through one spiritual lesson after another until the wheat is separated from the chaff and we've been refined.

I've learned to redefine happiness too. Happiness is not the lack of problems or pain. Happiness is surrendering to every feeling that comes along and being at peace with what is, even if I'm feeling white-hot rage. I've noticed something surprising. Often the people who have lost the most are the happiest after they get through their grief. That's because they dropped their illusions about life and learned to accept life on life's terms.

Embrace your destiny. Learn what true happiness is. It's okay to get angry and even enraged with your Higher Power. It's a personal relationship, and if you didn't get upset from time to time, then you're probably not being honest and real.

This program isn't going to turn you into some weird geek. It's going to polish and refine you. It's absolutely okay to be who you are. That's who you were created to be. Love, trust, and cherish that person, the unique piece of divinity you are. God created you with your gifts and strengths, your flaws and imperfections. Everything about you has been thoughtfully designed by the Creator, and you're a true work of art. There's a plan for your life. Don't worry about what it is. As they say in the program, *More shall be revealed.* You'll know what you need to know when it's time.

Activity

Sign an unconditional agreement to turn your will and life over to the care of God, a contract like you'd sign for any other legal arrangement. Words are powerful. They can create and heal, or destroy and hurt. In this activity, you have an opportunity to sign an agreement committing to work the Third Step. Fill in the blanks and then sign and date it. But don't sign it unless you mean it. Sooner or later, you'll be asked to make good on your words.

Agreement to Surrender to Destiny and Turn My Life and Will Over to the Care of God as I Understand Him

I, _____ [print name], on this _____ day of _____, 20_____, make an unconditional agreement with my Higher Power, God as I understand God, to turn my life and will over to His care. Although I may experience days when I would like to take back my life and will, or function by self-will, I understand those don't negate this Agreement. I understand that I may also experience problems, losses, and pain as part of my destiny, and that I may become angry with God for letting those problems occur when He had the power to stop them. I agree to work through my anger and continue surrendering to my Higher Power.

Activity (cont.)

I also commit to trusting God, clarifying that trusting Him doesn't mean I won't have pain and problems to endure. I understand that blessings will befall me too. I agree to accept this arrangement and my recovery as a package deal containing pleasant and unpleasant feelings and events.

I will verbally and mentally reinforce this Agreement by reading it, or reminding myself of it, as often as needed. I know I am never alone, even though it may appear that I am. I understand I may have to start over again, more than once, beginning various life circumstances in new settings and with new people as my life changes and I grow and require new lessons, or as losses occur. I agree to take care of myself the best that I can.

I thank God for taking on this job, realizing that at times, He will have His hands full guiding and caring for me and helping me fulfill His purpose and plan. I understand that details of my destiny will be shown to me at the right time, but I acknowledge that where I am now is where I'm meant to be. I also ask that God help me understand His will for me clearly and in a way that I can grasp.

Signed: _____

Dated: _____

This arrangement calls for a celebration. You may want to honor this agreement and working the first three Steps by having a quiet night alone with your Higher Power, by doing something special you want to do, or by spending an evening in quiet contemplation of what you've done. Or you may want to go out and have some fun.

Take a little longer break than usual. You have a job ahead in the next lesson, as you tackle your Fourth and Fifth Steps. Don't move forward until you feel rested, clear, and ready to do some intense work.

You're a Keeper

"Most of us have been so busy responding

to other people's problems that we haven't had time to

identify, much less take care of, our own problems."

—Codependent No More

Suggested reading: chapter 4, "Codependent Characteristics"

STEP FOUR: *Made a searching and fearless moral inventory of ourselves.*

STEP FIVE: *Admitted to God, to ourselves, and to another human being the exact nature of our wrongs.*

—from the TWELVE STEPS OF CO-DEPENDENTS ANONYMOUS

T he bondage of codependency made me so crazy that all those around me suffered greatly."

"My behavior made my husband's condition worse, but I felt like he deserved it."

"I still wanted to control things while my spouse was in treatment, because, after all, I had always taken care of everything."

"I caught myself answering for my spouse in Family Program. I started to realize that I was a big part of the problem."

"My tunnel vision into my husband's behaviors really damaged my family with neglect and irrational behavior on my part."

"I realized that although I was saying I wanted my spouse to get better, I was really afraid of getting better and looking at my own stuff. I kept adding pressure as a way of sabotaging."

"I wanted to be a victim. I continued to act like I did not have choices and that it was always everyone else's fault in the family for how I felt and reacted."

More Than Meets the Eye

The above quotes came from spouses of alcoholics when their husbands were in treatment, and when they got honest about who they really were and how they really felt. We can look so good on the outside. If we compare ourselves to the addict or alcoholic, we can look great next to him or her. But if we take a closer look, the codependents play a part too. Often when they take their inventory, that part is bigger than they thought. Can you be as searching, fearless, and honest as the women above?

You're about to find out.

Set a Date

Some Steps in Twelve Step programs are meant to be worked consecutively, like the trio of the first three. These next two are almost like one Step, and are meant to immediately follow each other (they also belong to a group of six, three groups of two that include Steps Four through Nine). Some people suggest setting an appointment to work Step Five with a trusted person—a sponsor, clergyperson or rabbi, or a counselor—before you begin work on Step Four. The person you choose to hear your Fifth Step needs to be someone who's completely trustworthy. Start work on the next two Steps by searching for who that person is.

You want more than someone who takes confessions. The ideal? Find someone trained in listening to Fifth Steps. Although you're doing the work, the abilities of the person you select make a difference in the level of success you achieve working your Fourth and Fifth Steps.

How well you work Steps Four and Five greatly impacts your recovery's foundation. Please choose your Fifth Step person carefully. Set the appointment to tell "another person, God, and yourself the exact nature of your wrongs" for four to six weeks from the date you actually begin writing your Fourth Step. You don't want to set the appointment so close to beginning your Fourth Step that you're rushed and do an incomplete job. You also don't want so much time to pass between working Steps Four and Five that you're walking around with emotional junk saturating your body and mind. After you finish your Fourth Step, you'll want to immediately clear the air.

Activity

1 Locating someone to listen to your Fifth Step may take some work. It's better to take your time and find a qualified person, one you feel good about, than to hurry and later regret your choice. Ask people in recovery groups for recommendations. Call a local treatment center and ask for referrals or suggestions. You may want to meet with this person before making a choice to see how you feel in that person's presence. Don't be afraid to acknowledge that this person isn't right for you, even if you searched hard to find him or her. Don't be afraid to ask questions. It's better to start your search over than to take this Step with someone who doesn't feel right. You'll know when you find him or her. Ask how many Fifth Steps this person has heard. That makes a difference. Also ask what program or programs the person is used to and most comfortable working with. Get someone who's experienced in the program you're working. Ask how far ahead this person recommends setting the appointment from the time you begin your Fourth Step work. I can't stress enough how important it is not only to do a thorough and fearless search in your inventory, but also to search thoroughly and fearlessly for the person who'll listen to your Fifth Step. Remember, you're not in this alone. You'll be guided. Something

Activity (cont.)

Activity (cont.)

else to consider is cost. Find out if this person charges and, if so, how much. Can you afford it? I've not had to pay for a Fifth Step yet, but our world is changing. Even if the person doesn't charge, if you use a clergyperson or rabbi, consider leaving a donation. Before you choose the person to hear your Fifth Step, consider that person's gender. Will you feel more at ease with a man or woman? While you'll be guided in your search, you still need to do your part, and your part may require hard work.

While it may appear easiest to have another Twelve Step program member or your sponsor listen to your Fifth Step, that can be dangerous. The person may relapse or otherwise break confidentiality more readily than a trained professional would. Be careful whom you take your Fifth Step with because if this person breaks confidentiality by repeating anything you confided, it could hurt you, your reputation, and your confidence in Twelve Step recovery.

When you locate the right person to hear your Fifth Step, ask if he or she prefers you do your Fourth Step a particular way or if you should figure that out yourself. If your Fifth Step person or the Twelve Step groups you attend suggest using a formula other than what's offered in this workbook, then you'll need to choose the formula that works best for you. It may be the one that feels best, or it could be the one you most resist.

Activity (cont.)

❷ Choose a date to begin writing your inventory. Consider when you'll have time to devote to writing daily for at least two weeks, maybe longer. When you're clear about whom you want to listen to your Fifth Step and when you'll begin work on your Fourth Step, make an appointment to take your Fifth Step that lines up closely with when you'll be done with your inventory. Then stick to the schedule. Don't take less than two weeks or more than six weeks to do your Fourth Step work. Your Fifth Step person may suggest how much time to take doing your Fourth Step. But please be sure you have an appointment scheduled to take your Fifth Step before you begin your inventory work. After you set the dates, the clock is ticking. That's good. You're about to get acquainted with your new best friend—yourself.

Inventory Formats

Step Four reads, "Made a searching and fearless moral inventory of ourselves." The action in this step is *making*. We make the inventory by using paper and a pen or pencil, a typewriter, or a computer. We create it, make it. The Step doesn't say, "Think about an inventory in your head."

The words *searching and fearless moral inventory* sound severe and open-ended. What are you fearlessly searching for? Exactly how do you search, and when is that search complete? You'll know. It'll break your heart open like someone pounding a coconut with a hammer. It'll work, and you'll feel done.

The purpose of this Step is to see what we have, for better and for worse. We want to look at our habits, emotions, behaviors, and the beliefs that create our behaviors. We look for specific things we've done that we're ashamed of and for our good points and good deeds. You can also begin family-of-origin work. I've included a sample format so you can get an idea of how to do this.

You can make an inventory many different ways. This lesson will describe a few of them. Read through the lesson, and then choose one from what's offered by your group, your Fifth Step person, this book, or any other books you've read.

Here's the key to the Fourth and Fifth Steps. There are one or two needles in the codependency haystack that you're fearlessly searching for. They're those secrets that you feel guiltiest about, the things you would prefer to take to your grave.

Although some things are private, *We're only as sick as our secrets* is another program slogan that's accurate, for the most part. Look for anything that causes you to feel bad about yourself, any habitual behaviors you do that create negative consequences. We want a clear picture of ourselves.

Inventorying ourselves is complex. It's not like inventorying items at a grocery store. Review the following examples carefully.

Inventory from a List of Emotions, Beliefs, and Codependent Behaviors

One way to inventory yourself is to go through the following list of emotions, beliefs, and behaviors associated with codependency. Mark which ones you feel, believe, or do and write about the ways these tendencies manifest in your life now. Include the first time you remember feeling that way, or believing that belief, or when the behavior first began. Rate each item listed on a scale from one to ten, with one being the least and ten being the most, for how much of a problem that feeling, belief, or behavior causes now, and indicate with a check mark the ones that are most problematic now.

Then end the inventory by making a list of positive emotions, beliefs, behaviors, assets, or skills that you possess.

For both negative and positive parts of your inventory, write notes about specific incidents that demonstrate or show how you act out these emotions, beliefs, behaviors, and assets. End the inventory by listing some traits that you'd like to acquire.

To make it less confusing, following is what your inventory pages should look like. After these sample headings, you'll find a list of possible codependent traits to choose from, including feelings, beliefs, and behaviors. You may have others besides what's on that list. To begin this inventory format, divide a piece of paper the long way into six columns by drawing lines. Then use the following as headings, filling in the area below each heading. Or use these columns as a guide to write about each line item in "story" form.

Negative Emotions, Beliefs, and Behaviors from My Past (Include Names of Any Other Person Involved)	Original Incident That Triggered That Feeling, Belief, or Behavior, and the Approximate Age I Was or the Date When It Occurred	How It Manifests in My Life Now (Be Specific)	Rate Pain on a Scale of 1 to 10 (1 Hurts Least and 10 Hurts Most)	Priorities— Mark with an "X"	Notes—Include Examples That Show What I Do Now

After you inventory negative assets and the specific wrongs you've done, here are categories for the positive side of your inventory. Again, you can either divide a piece of paper into four columns or write about these items in story form. Choose from beliefs or behaviors such as caring, loving, kind, encouraging, creative, having good boundaries, intelligent, curious, calm, good in a crisis, or any other positive quality or skill you possess. Yes, you do have some.

Positive Assets, Including Emotions, Beliefs, Behaviors, and Skills I Possess	When and Why This First Occurred	Specific Examples, Including Things Others Have Said and How I Feel about This	Other Comments

Now, look at what you'd like to acquire. Maybe you know someone who models behaviors you'd like to have. Use your imagination. (If you put half as much energy into working on developing yourself as you've done obsessing about someone or something, you can have almost anything you want.)

Positive Assets, Attributes, Emotions, Beliefs, Behaviors, and Skills I'd Like to Acquire, Obtain, Get Better At	What I Could Do to Help Get This Started	Why I Want This (Motive)	How I Envision Myself Feeling, Looking, or Living

Scan the following list of possible emotions, beliefs, and behaviors. If, during the process of scanning the list, the memory of an incident or an emotion is triggered, whether it's connected to the list or not, stop scanning and begin writing about the memory or emotion that became triggered. Try to get to the root of the emotion, belief, or behavior that triggered the memory or emotion. Inventorying ourselves isn't an intellectual process. It's experiential, and it's emotional too. It begins a process—which life will continue organically—of getting rid of what we don't want in order to make room for what we want to acquire, and who we want to become.

EMOTIONS

Feel afraid people will reject me

Feel alone

Feel annoyed and irritated by most people and life

Feel anxiety

Feel as though I'm a burden to others

Feel as though my life isn't real

Feel ashamed of having a problem and needing help (codependency or other problem)

Feel ashamed of my family

Feel ashamed of myself

Feel betrayed

Feel blame toward myself

Feel blame toward others

Feel blame toward others for my behavior

Feel blame toward others for my unhappiness

Feel depressed

Feel different from other people (in a negative way)

Feel disapproving of myself

Feel disapproving of others

Feel dislike or hatred for others

Feel dissatisfied with life

Feel drained by my relationships

Feel entitled to everything I want even if I don't work for it

Feel exhausted and depleted

Feel fear

Feel guilty

Feel hopeless and helpless

Feel incompetent

Feel invisible

Feel judged by other people

Feel lethargic

Feel like a failure (at almost everything)

Feel like I don't belong (no matter where I am)

EMOTIONS (cont.)

Feel like I'm always in the wrong place doing something wrong

Feel like I'm on the wrong track

Feel like I'm deprived of whatever I want or of anything good

Feel like my life hasn't begun yet

Feel lonely

Feel overly concerned with how others perceive me (try to control their perception of me)

Feel overwhelmed with grief

Feel overwhelming need to control people and situations to keep from getting hurt

Feel resentment

Feel sad

Feel self-hatred

Feel sense of dread

Feel separate from others

Feel separated from God

Feel so much fear I have panic attacks

Feel terrified of leaving the house

Feel terrified of making people angry

Feel trapped

Feel undeserving (of anything good)

Feel unfulfilled

Feel unhappy

Feel unloved and unlovable

Feel used

Feel victimized

BELIEFS

Believe I can't be direct

Believe I can't make good decisions

Believe I can't financially take care of myself

Believe I can't trust myself

Believe I don't have a life

Believe I have no assets or strengths

Believe I have no purpose

Believe I have no skills

Believe I know what's best for others

Believe I need someone to take care of me or be with me

Believe I'll lose all self-esteem if I admit to making a mistake

Believe I'm alone in the world

Believe I'm always right

Believe I'm always wrong

Believe I'm better than others

Believe I'm fat although others tell me I'm not

Believe I'm incapable of dealing with anger

Believe I'm incapable of solving my problems

BELIEFS (cont.)

Believe I'm not as good as others

Believe I'm not creative

Believe I'm not enough or not good enough

Believe I'm not responsible for myself

Believe I'm responsible for other people's feelings and behaviors

Believe I'm trapped

Believe I'm ugly

Believe I'm unable to care for myself or live/be alone (not in a romantic relationship)

Believe I'm unable to learn anything new

Believe I'm undesirable and unattractive

Believe I'm unforgivable

Believe I'm unloved and unlovable

Believe my emotions are wrong or bad

Believe my entire life is wrong

Believe other people owe me

Believe others hold the key to my happiness

Believe that how family members and those close to me behave is a direct reflection of my self-worth

Believe who I am isn't okay

BEHAVIORS

Am abusing another person (emotionally, physically, sexually)

Am controlled by someone else

Am defensive

Am dependent on people (in an unhealthy way)

Am dogmatic and inflexible

Am easily manipulated

Am experiencing sexual problems (can't say no, am impotent, am frigid, have sex when I don't want to, feel repulsed by sex)

Am flat (no emotions)

Am having an affair or affairs

Am indecisive

Am needy and clingy

Am not aware of my emotions

Am not in touch with my true powers and abilities

Am overly focused on others

Am out of touch with myself

Am passive-aggressive (I don't deal openly with anger, but I get even eventually)

Am surrounded by people I don't like but fear letting go of them

Am tense and rigid

Am trapped and looking for an escape

Am unable to express who I am—or have great difficulty expressing myself

93

BEHAVIORS (cont.)

Am unable to receive

Am without goals

Annoy others intentionally

Attempt to control other people

Can't handle reality

Compare myself to others

Compulsively engage in sexual behaviors

Confuse pain with love

Constantly deny what I know inside is true

Deprive myself unnecessarily

Display inappropriate emotional affect or responses

Don't ask directly for what I want and need (hint, sigh, manipulate)

Don't deal with anger—other people's or mine

Don't feel good about myself

Don't know how to be intimate

Don't know how to connect with my Higher Power

Don't know how to connect with my purpose

Don't know how to connect with people

Don't know how to nurture others

Don't know what I think of others or how I feel about them

Exercise heavy, repressive control of myself

Fantasize about another person's death

Fantasize about dying (myself)

Feel hurt, abandoned

Find it almost impossible to say no

Find it difficult to have fun or enjoy myself—I can't let loose

Frequently become sick

Get caught up in perfectionism

Give compulsively

Go to any lengths to stop people from becoming angry with me

Have an aggressive, angry response to life and events

Have been or am now being abused (emotionally, physically, sexually)

Have difficulty being alone

Have lost faith in God and life

Have no ambition

Have no self-awareness

Have no sense of self

Have not received nurturing

Have a passive response to life and events

Have poor communication skills

Have problems with eating disorders

Have sex to cover emotions

Have violent explosions of emotions

Hope and wait for someone else's death so I'll be happy and free

Judge myself

BEHAVIORS (cont.)

Judge others

Justify my behaviors

Lack boundaries—don't set limits about how far people can go for or with me

Lack boundaries—don't set limits as to how far I go with or for others

Lack self-esteem

Lack a sense of humor

Lack spontaneity

Let others use me for money

Make excuses for others

Manipulate

Need distractions to prevent me from looking at my life

Need external validation

Obsess

Often believe lies

Over-apologize for myself when it's unnecessary

Over-commit

Over-indulge myself

People-please

Plan revenge

Prefer it when there's a crisis or problem to solve

Punish someone by spending their money irresponsibly

Repress or ignore my feelings

Resort to denial

Try to control the flow of events

Try to have power where I don't

Use food to medicate emotions or find good feelings

Use medication or alcohol to smooth emotions

Use other people for money

Was legitimately victimized as a child or adult

Wish I were dead

Won't admit to wrongdoing

Create a Family-of-Origin Work Chart

Here's another alternative for your inventory. It's a family-of-origin chart. I've filled in a few lines just to spark some ideas. Don't get caught up in perfectionism. Take a basic inventory of the ways you've been affected by your past, by events that took place, and by some losses you went through when you didn't know how to deal with your emotions or didn't have enough safety or support to grieve. Here's the sample chart:

Original Incident	Feelings about It	Belief Created	Today's Behavior
Molested by the husband of a family I babysat for when I was eleven. Then frequently sexually and emotionally abused by family members after that.	Shame, fear, traumatized, self-hatred, feel like I'm no good.	I'm a bad person; something is wrong with me—something that cannot be fixed; I deserve bad things; I confuse love and sex.	Initiate relationships with abusive men; act from feelings of shame, low self-worth, or confusion about sex; no boundaries—don't know what appropriate boundaries are.
Father left home when I was three, didn't say goodbye; I rarely saw him again.	Abandoned, unlovable, sad, grief.	I'm not lovable; I'm undesirable; I have to make people like me or they'll leave; everyone I love goes away.	Spend too much money on clothes and appearance; try to control people so they won't leave; clingy and needy; relationships controlled by fear of abandonment instead of by how I feel about the person.
Started drinking at age twelve when I came home from school to eat lunch. Nobody there; snuck shots from whiskey bottle under the kitchen sink.	First connection with good feelings I had; I didn't care that I didn't feel like I fit in.	Alcohol and drugs are the answer. They help me stay in control of how I feel and my pain. I'm good-for-nothing, like my father. Later, I'm a bad person for drinking and using drugs.	Alcoholic and addict until I went into remission. Needed to forgive myself. Took most of my life to realize that drinking and using drugs may have saved my life.

96

Do a Confession-Style Inventory

Another approach is to look at the list and then write in a free-flow story form about your life and the things you've done that you feel bad about. Include things you don't want to do anymore and secrets you've kept that cause you to repress your emotions. Treat your inventory like a confession—a time to admit your wrongdoings. But please remember that not treating yourself with love and respect is a moral defect too.

Recreating Yourself

"Even after recognizing my codependency and decreasing or stopping some of my cognitions and behaviors, I still didn't feel whole for a long time," said Pira M., a woman recovering from codependency who also works as a therapist. "I'd just changed my object of codependency from my husband to various other people who would allow me to become codependent with them, such as my children, parents, and others. Becoming aware of this helped me realize that I had been a codependent for a long time, and I just kept repeating the cycle," she said.

"With more soul-searching, I discovered an underlying assumption by which I live: I am not good enough. Other beliefs or life themes have included not measuring up to others, not being popular, not being wanted or desired, not being able to do anything right, not ever significantly impacting anything, and being a late bloomer.

"Perhaps if we discover our assumptions or beliefs about ourselves," Pira said, "we'd have the opportunity to change the undesirable ones."

She's correct. You can't put water in a glass that's already full. We need to get rid of the old to make room for the new.

By now, you've gotten a glimpse that this work may be difficult. It's easier to suffer if we know it's for a good cause. There's an important, crucial reason for doing this work. You're identifying and getting rid of the old things that hold you back to make room for life to deliver good stuff to you.

One other idea to keep in mind is our impressive ability to justify what we do. By looking clearly and closely at ourselves, we can drop our justifications and truly clean our side of the street.

"I have always thought that one of the big, big deals with the Twelve Steps (which I've worked in AA for twenty-one years and in Al-Anon for two) is the ability—or inability—to be honest with myself, especially when it comes to being honest about 'my part,'" said A. J., another woman recovering from codependency. "I'm always amazed by my ability to justify why I do what I do, like when something triggers old emotions and I respond out of proportion. I feel crazy for feeling the way I do."

Remember, you're not crazy; you're codependent. By doing this work, one day your behaviors will make sense to you. Something will click. Behaviors that have baffled you for years, made you feel crazy, or caused you guilt can suddenly make complete sense. When it happens, we forgive ourselves. Don't try to make this awareness happen. *Let* it happen. That's what we're learning to do. Despite all the things we may have done or that other people did to us, we truly can trust God, ourselves, and life.

Think of this as a treasure hunt—and you are the gold.

It will take many sittings to complete a thorough, complete inventory. Create a comfortable space to do your work. Each time, before beginning, say a prayer to your Higher Power asking for guidance and help. Light a candle. Ensure you have privacy and a calm environment so you can hear yourself think. Then fearlessly go searching and make a thorough inventory of you.

Activity

Choose which format you're going to use from the examples in this book, and choose the person who's going to listen to your Fifth Step. Ask that person for suggestions, and ask your recovery group too. Then agree on the date for your Fifth Step. Now you're ready to start your Fourth Step inventory.

Look at How Strong You've Become

It's easy to see how people, places, and things from our past have harmed us. It's harder and takes focus to see the good that we've gained from our experiences. But there is good, and plenty of it. People from alcoholic or dysfunctional families seem to do better in stressful times than most people, and they can handle hard times and heavy workloads on the job when other people fold. Their pasts have made them stronger and more reliable than other people who haven't had it as hard.

After we finish our Fourth and Fifth Steps and get all the junk out, we can start seeing ourselves in a new light. We can start looking at our families and our pasts differently. Who's to say we didn't get exactly what we needed to make us healers, teachers, or whatever and whoever we've become—or who we're going to be?

You'll know when you're finished with your inventory and Steps Four through Nine. You'll be able to look at your past with peace. People say we can't change the past, but that's not true. We can change it by how we perceive it, and whether we use it to become and stay victims, or to show ourselves how strong we are. We don't diminish or trivialize tragedies such as abuse and other things that no human being should have to go through. The goal of this work is to feel everything we need to feel that we didn't feel before, and then to release the emotions, forgive other people and ourselves so we can love and respect ourselves, and feel confident in our ability to love other people too.

Be aware that as you do this inventory and look back at your past, you may feel depressed until you go in for your Fifth Step. That's why it's important to have the appointment set. Try not to take your feelings too seriously if a lot of difficult emotions come up. It's like when we clean house—things look worse for a while, because we've piled up all the dirt and the mess. We create chaos to make space for order to set in.

If the emotions get too hard to handle, talk to someone while you're waiting for the date of your Fifth Step. Another one of our shortcomings may be that we don't ask for the help we need because we don't want to burden anyone. We think we should be able to handle everything by ourselves, no matter how hard it is or how bad we feel. But if you need support or just an evening out with a friend, ask. Don't ask from the standpoint of being a victim who needs taking care of. Don't demand or manipulate. But do ask, as one healthy adult asking another for help.

Activity

1. Begin a journal. If you decide to do a thorough Fourth and Fifth Step again—which many people do the second or third year they're in recovery—it will be helpful if you start writing in a journal a couple of times each week. Record your beliefs, observations, old feelings that come up from the past, and new beliefs you become aware of. You might think that, when you're going through a problem, you'll always remember how bad you felt, but it will pass and likely become a distant memory. So write about it while it's fresh. Get in the habit of writing in a journal regularly. It'll keep things moving through you so you won't get emotionally stuck.

2. Remember how you feel while you're working on this Step. Write in a journal about it. By doing so, you can be of assistance to others when they do their Fourth and Fifth Steps.

Admit to God, Yourself, and Someone Else Exactly What You Did

Step Five is powerful. You'll receive powerful results if you're thorough in your work. Many of us, because we don't believe it's okay to be who we are, aren't used to being gut-level honest with ourselves, other people, and God, so we stay trapped in the past.

It's said that Joan of Arc, before taking her warriors into battle, had them get down on their knees, confess their wrongdoings, and ask God to forgive them. She was an intelligent woman and guided by God. When we're carrying guilt, we believe we deserve to be punished. She knew her warriors wouldn't do their best on the battlefields if they went to war with guilt and remorse inside them. They needed forgiveness first.

Look at this as a sacred time in your life when you're cleansing your heart and soul, getting rid of old emotions, wounds, mistakes, guilt—the things that can hold you back from feeling joy and experiencing success. Be gentle with yourself until the day comes when you go in for your Fifth Step. Then, be as honest as possible. If you're lucky, the person listening to your Step will help guide you. You can get the very worst, most painful things off your chest, and just let them go—be done with them. If possible, write down the words that person says at the end—especially any good qualities he or she observes in you. You may hang on to these words for the rest of your life. I did. They can be exactly what you need to hear.

After taking your Fifth Step, you may feel many pounds lighter. But some people don't get an immediate sense of relief. It may also take time for the emotions and guilt to lift. Recovery isn't the same for everyone. If you don't feel like a brand-new person the second you've finished, it doesn't mean you did it wrong, or didn't do it well enough. Give yourself time.

Also, other incidents, emotions, or beliefs you forgot may come up after you do your Fifth Step. Often, these can be important issues that you also need to get off your chest. If that happens, make a follow-up appointment and finish.

Remember, while you're taking your Fifth Step, that you're not just telling another person about yourself. You're telling God and yourself too. When you finish, go someplace where you can be by yourself for some quiet time to talk to God, look at your past, and see yourself with eyes of forgiveness and love. This is who you are, where you've been, and what you've done. It's your journey so far.

As one woman said, "Everything—every dirty little detail of my life—was meant to be and can be used for good."

You've just finished one of the hardest, bravest things you will ever be asked to do. Know you're loved by God. You're deep into the journey of learning to love other people and yourself. No matter what happened in your past or what you did to protect yourself, you don't need survival behaviors anymore. You're safe now.

A rich journey awaits you. You'll see and do wonderful things. You're in the midst of becoming transformed. You'll still be you, but the gold will shine more, and the rust and flaws will either become a beautiful part of you, you'll let go of them, or they'll be turned over, and you'll use those parts for good. The defects will be turned into assets that help others and ultimately help you.

But it's not over yet. Just as Steps Four and Five go together, so do Steps Six and Seven. The two pairs couple together. They may not be the stairway to heaven, but they're the stairway to self-love and love for others. These four Steps—Four, Five, Six, and Seven—are a unit unto themselves. They also go with another couplet, Steps Eight and Nine.

Before you go to sleep the evening after you take your Fifth Step, even though you may be exhausted, you have two more Steps to work.

The action you'll take is different. Easier. The grueling and hard work is done. But it's critical that you follow up Step Five with Steps Six and Seven. So drive directly home, or to someplace where it's quiet and you can be alone. If you have to sleep, eat, or go to work first, then that's what you must do. But if it's at all possible, go directly to some place quiet and private, and work the next two Steps.

Before you close this lesson, put behaviors from Steps Four and Five in your tool kit. Make this the beginning of stopping your obsessive focus on others and the start of self-awareness. Of all the emotions, guilt is the worst. As you go through the days, months, and years to come, you will make mistakes. Things will come up that you'll feel guilty about—sometimes so guilty you'll feel paralyzed, like you can never hold your head up high again. I know people who've felt that way. I've felt that way too. When it's necessary, look at what you've done wrong, your defects, or behaviors that create guilt. Then pick up the phone or meet with a friend, and tell somebody else what you've done.

Activity

1. *Take your own inventory.* That means keep your side of the street clean. Some people call it "looking at and taking responsibility for our part." But it's easy for people with codependency to take this too far. We stop looking at other people entirely, and what they're doing and how it affects us. Before long, we can find ourselves living with a spouse who's cheating, who's lying to us, who may be a practicing alcoholic, or who's financially irresponsible, and the entire time we're oblivious. Why? We're looking at our part, what we did wrong, or what we did to create this. We don't have to take these inventory Steps that far. Sometimes our part is denying how much someone else's behavior hurts, and then finally setting the limits we need to set to take care of ourselves.

2. Other times we don't see our mistakes. Remember, no human being is perfect; we're not made that way. Our flaws are built in; we come with lessons to learn embedded in our DNA. Keep your eyes on the goal of recovery: to live fully in the present moment, trusting and taking responsibility for yourself. Life is to be lived. If we're not making mistakes, we're not alive.

3. If you still feel plugged up with old emotions and the residue from your Fifth Step after you complete Steps Six and Seven, do some exercise. Work out. Start taking long walks. Sometimes getting our body moving gets those old emotions and feelings, including guilt, moving out of us and into the waste dump for the universe.

You've done a great job, you've shown commitment to the program, and, most of all, you've shown commitment to loving and taking care of yourself. There are promises attached to doing this work, benefits you'll soon see. Now, as discussed earlier, go home, pick up the workbook, and go directly to Lesson Six. You may feel tired, disoriented, emotionally drained. But you can do the next lesson anyway. You'll get the strength you need. You're about to renew your connection to yourself, your Higher Power, and others in a new way. You'll look back at this someday and say it's the most worthwhile work you've ever done. I hope you feel as good about yourself as I do. I know how hard it is. I don't know your name—we may or may not meet someday. But we're in this fellowship together, and I'm extremely proud of you.

Ready?

"... God has exciting,

interesting things in store for each of us.

I believe there is an enjoyable,

worthwhile purpose—besides taking care of people and

being an appendage to someone—for each of us."

—Codependent No More

Suggested reading: chapter 10, "Live Your Own Life"

STEP SIX: Were entirely ready to have God remove all these defects of character.

STEP SEVEN: Humbly asked God to remove our shortcomings.

—from the TWELVE STEPS OF CO-DEPENDENTS ANONYMOUS

Steps Six and Seven are my favorite. They're magical. They are the keys that unlock our initial transformation. The first time we work the Steps, we will experience the rewards of our efforts. Later, they are every bit as magical when we use them as daily tools for just about anything we can't handle, which can often mean just about everything that happens to and in us, and the things we feel.

If we've been given a magical wand, these two Steps—used together exactly as they read—are it. They're the Steps that we climb that take us from who we've been to who we're going to become.

If you look at the action we are required to take, these Steps call for the easiest work on our part: *were entirely ready* and *humbly asked.* It can't be more simple than that. Yet many people in Twelve Step programs report having a common fear. *If I ask God to take away my shortcomings—and God does—there won't be anything left. I'll disappear.*

That belief is a trick we play on ourselves, our way of resisting change and transformation. "We"—the person we recognize as "our real self"—isn't going anywhere. You're not going to disappear. It's closer to how a sculptor works when he's sculpting an image of a person. He starts with a block of clay. Then he carefully removes everything that isn't needed. What the sculptor is left with is the most necessary substance to form his creation.

Be not afraid. What you'll have after working these Steps—in the days, months, and years to follow—will be more like the real you than you've ever been before.

If you have some fears about taking these two Steps, stand back a little. Take a realistic look at the process you've been experiencing. Nothing that you've been asked to do will harm or diminish you. The codependency is what took your soul. It's where you lost yourself. By doing these two Steps immediately after taking your Fifth Step, you'll begin the discovery process of learning who you are.

Activity

Do you have any fears about working these two Steps? Go to the top of page 107. Read them. Does anything put a knot in your stomach, or make your hands tremble? Do you have any resistance to taking these Steps? All you need to do is say what your fears are, admit them to yourself. Ask yourself and answer honestly, *Am I ready to go to the next level of the stairway by taking these two Steps?*

Good News

The sweetest, most calming part of these Steps—and you'll see it if you read them closely—is that although we call recovery *self-help*, absolutely nothing in these two Steps says anything about pulling ourselves up by our bootstraps, using will or force to change, or even using the concept we've come to call *self-help*. These two Steps could not make it clearer that we don't change ourselves. Our Higher Power changes us. What a relief to people caught in addictions, or compulsive behavior patterns. All we do is become entirely ready to let go of the beliefs, emotions, and behaviors that we're calling *defects of character*. When it comes to codependency, we're talking particularly about the survival behaviors we relied on to help us feel safe.

But remember, those survival behaviors, such as control, are illusions. They don't protect us. They turn on us and make us feel crazy. The tricky part is that we may have convinced ourselves we need them. For instance, we may believe that if we stay resentful or angry at someone, we don't have to worry about letting that person in, or letting that person hurt us. If we let go of our anger or bitterness and let the love flow through us, what will keep us from getting back in a relationship we know isn't good for us again?

The answer is, we'll learn new behaviors; we're about to begin "college." In this particular situation, because we love ourselves, we'll set appropriate boundaries. We may have to go through a course similar to a college class. The difference is, the school is our life. As I wrote earlier in this workbook, just about anyone can become a teacher for setting boundaries—even the person who's making us crazy or not treating us respectfully. Maybe it's that person we obsessed about for years. He or she gave us just enough to keep us hooked in, but not enough to have a fulfilling relationship. Then finally we crossed the threshold, got into a relationship with the person, and discovered we didn't want to be with him or her after all. We got tricked into obsessing about and wanting someone because it was something we couldn't have. We got so busy obsessing about how the other person felt about us that we didn't take time to see how we felt about him or her—or if we really enjoyed being with that person.

That's one of the greatest dangers of obsession. It can be a red herring, a distraction from looking at situations realistically and seeing the situation clearly. All we see when we're obsessed is that we want something or someone we don't have.

I am not saying it's wrong to have goals or to pursue what we want. I'm not advocating that tired-out theory *Be careful what you ask for because you might get it.* Ask for the best in your life. If you honestly and thoroughly work these Steps, that's what you'll get.

Again, you'll be called on to trust your Higher Power, the God of your understanding. God is the one who'll be changing you. You can relax into your life and into the arms of your Higher Power.

Following your Fifth Step, find a quiet, serene place where you can be by yourself. Now, I'm basing how to work these Steps on Alcoholics Anonymous, the original version and suggested way of working these steps. This isn't my own creation. As suggested in the Big Book, get down on your knees. If that isn't physically possible, you can always get down on your knees in spirit.

It's time to have a heart-to-heart discussion, but it's not yet time to talk to God. The first discussion is the one you're going to have with yourself.

Are you ready to let go of your survival behaviors, your habitual codependent behaviors that you may have made a way of life? Are you ready to let God, in His wisdom and timing, remove your low self-worth? Remember how you told yourself that the reason bad things happened was because you were a bad person? Are you ready to let go of that character defect, to let God take it?

God may not just swoop down and in one moment remove these things. Most likely, you'll go through experiences that will (1) make you aware of the behavior or defect, (2) help you accept that it's a behavior you no longer need or want to use, and (3) help you change. Either you will learn how to reverse a negative behavior into a positive quality, or you will be given some options.

Becoming ready to change is a process. This is the true beginning of changing your codependent behaviors.

Are you ready to open your mouth and talk directly? Ready to say who you are and what you want instead of hemming and hawing? Ready to be alone instead of being in a relationship with someone who makes you miserable? Ready to be financially responsible for yourself? Be prepared for how long it takes to become financially responsible. We work toward freedom and self-responsibility. While we may have complained about being controlled and held back by someone we've been in a relationship with, it can be convenient to blame someone else for where we're at and for our misery. It can be scary taking responsibility—true responsibility—for our happiness, our life, our sense of self-fulfillment, and our choices. But what's scarier is not changing and feeling victimized for the rest of our lives.

Are you ready to truly turn all of you over to your Creator—God as you understand God—and let Him decide what your defects are and what, how, and when they'll be taken from you?

You've worked so hard, come so far. I cannot make this choice for you. But if the answer is yes, or you're willing to become willing, then, if you can get on your knees—either physically or in spirit—do that. You can say a prayer of your own choosing to take the Seventh Step. Or you can use the following prayer, which I wrote, based on the prayer in *Alcoholics Anonymous*.

GOD, I'M WILLING *that you take all of me. I surrender myself to your care—body, mind, and soul—for however long I'm going to be here. I cannot change myself. I've tried for years and made a mess. Your love for me sees past that, and I thank you for that. I thank you for everything that's taken me from all the pain I've been in—the confusion, the lack of clarity— to this place where we're entering into an active partnership, with you shaping me into who I am to become.*

I realize I don't have to fear that I'll disappear or lose myself. The truth is, I've lost myself in all these past unhealthy relationships. I understand that this is an act of love on your part to help me find myself and discover who I really am. I pray now that you might take all of me—good and bad, defects and strengths—and use me in your service. I humbly ask that you might take my shortcomings and turn me into who you, in your omnipotence and wisdom, want me to become.

I thank you in advance. I also understand that at times this process may not be easy. I do ask for a favor. Sometimes, I don't understand things. Please be as gentle as possible with me, and show me what I am to do in a way that I understand. Let me feel your loving touch and be assured of your guidance.

Turn me into a warrior and a loving person, someone whom you can use in your kingdom to help others heal and to fulfill your plan for me. I trust you to fill in all the details of how I can best learn what I'm to learn, change what I'm to change, and be of the greatest service to you and others.

I thank you for all you've done for me up until now. I thank you in advance for what's coming. Take self-will and fear from me. Take financial insecurity and the fear that I cannot take care of myself. Help me to see myself a little bit at least the way you see me. Keep me on track. Let my will be aligned with yours, and remove anything that stands between them.

As much as I can, help me let go of my need to control and be in denial. Give me courage to face the truth. Reveal my purpose to me—why I'm here on earth, what you want me to do, and who you want me to be. More than anything, help me let go of desiring and wanting. Help me become an open channel of love, awareness, and healing for other people, so by my actions they will want to serve you too.

Help me let go of narcissism, vainglory, and seeking to be superior. Instead, let me be clear about who is the Master and who is the servant. All the days of my life, help me to remember that I'm not here to acquire things and power, but to be of loving service.

This prayer is just a suggestion for talking to your Higher Power. Use words of your choosing; they may be completely different. But be prepared now. For what you have done is ask God to put you in a refining process, filter out your defects, and let them be replaced by His loving, healing power.

You may be amazed at the lessons that begin—and how quickly they start. Sometimes you may barely catch your breath from one lesson when the next one begins, and the next one will be more challenging and harder. Remember, unnecessary pieces of clay will be removed. You're being sculpted, masterfully created into a new person.

One warning: It's easy to fall into the trap of thinking your life up until this moment hasn't mattered. That's inappropriate thinking. From the first breath you drew at birth until your lungs exhale your last, every moment of your life is important. It matters. Now you'll begin learning how to make every moment count.

Activity

You may be either energized or absolutely exhausted. What an experience! No matter how many Fourth and Fifth Steps you take, you'll likely always remember this as your best, your finest—because it is. Carefully put away all papers from your Fifth Step. These are private, for nobody's eyes but your own. I've watched people play games with this, leaving their written Step out so a spouse or parent could see it. That will likely cause pain and is part of a game. If you don't have a safe place, then burn it. It's not a bad idea to burn one copy of your Fourth Step while keeping another. (You'll need it to make your list of amends.) At the beginning of this workbook, I said these Steps are hard work. This is some of the hardest but most rewarding work you'll ever do. Before you go to bed, please put away all papers concerning your Fourth and Fifth Steps. Choose a place where it's completely impossible for anyone else to find your papers.

Then get a great night's sleep. This time, you'll want to take some time before you dive into the next Step. Don't push yourself too hard or fast into the next lesson. Make certain you're feeling renewed and ready to move on. Remember, in the first month after your Fifth Step, something else might come up that you need to get off your chest. If that happens, please take care of yourself accordingly. Set an appointment with a counselor or clergyperson and deal with it.

A Super-Tool

At the beginning of this lesson, I told you how much I loved these Steps, how grateful I am for them. These two little Steps alone should also be in your pocket or purse, ready to pull out and use on a moment's notice.

When a problem, a feeling, or an issue comes up that you can't handle, quickly repeat Steps Six and Seven. Ask God to help you become ready to let go of your anger, fear, "stuckness," financial instability, indecision, or yearning. Then ask God humbly to take it from you. I can't think of one problem you can't use this on. The key and the trick is becoming ready. For some reason, we like clinging to these defects.

Activity

Buy a plain, small notebook. Write Steps Six and Seven in it. Turn to these Steps whenever anything arises—whether it's your anger, your confusion, your need for direction, or a resentment. It doesn't have to be a huge problem. God cares about all parts of your life. Then write in the notebook about the issues you use these two Steps on. After identifying a problem, ask God to help you to become entirely ready to have Him remove the shortcoming. Then ask Him to take it from you—to remove it! Stay aware of what happens, for example, if a lesson begins or something else takes place. Do not try to control it. If you're going to try to do anything, try to surrender more deeply. This notebook can help you fall in love with these two little Steps too.

One afternoon, on the social networking site Facebook, I saw a beautiful prayer written by an anonymous person. I tried for weeks to find the author so I could attribute it to her, but I didn't have any luck. But although I can't claim this prayer as mine, I still want you to have it: "God, please show me what Step to work and when to work it." From this day on, that's going to be your guide. Meanwhile, take at least a week off to catch your balance and let what happened sink in. Don't be perfectionistic. It's not what these Steps ask us to do. The Twelve Step approach is *Progress not perfection.* Don't move forward too soon, but don't let too much time pass either before you turn the page in this book and move on to the next lesson.

Creating Self-Respect

"In love and dignity,

speak the truth—as we think, feel,

and know it—and it shall set us free."

—Codepentent No More

Suggested reading: chapter 17, "Communication"

STEP EIGHT: Made a list of all persons we had harmed and became willing to make amends to them all.

STEP NINE: Made direct amends to such people wherever possible, except when to do so would injure them or others.

—from the TWELVE STEPS OF CO-DEPENDENTS ANONYMOUS

Step Eight calls for two actions. One is "made a list." The other is "became willing." This Step doesn't say that we make amends to everyone on our list. But we become willing to do that. It's about surrendering resistance and developing a humble attitude. Step by Step, we become more closely aligned with our Higher Power's will. In Step Eight we show that we'll go to any length to learn to love ourselves and others and to have a healthy, functional life.

Most of us have been willing to stop at nothing to take care of others. This Step challenges us to go that far for ourselves and our spiritual growth. Steps Four through Nine are a series of pairs of Steps that, when properly worked, give us back a clean slate for our lives. Steps Eight and Nine provide the finishing touches.

A New Old You

Steps Four through Nine take us back to the past so we can see what happened to us, what we did to others, and how our past still affects us today. We also look for behaviors we don't want or need anymore, survival behaviors from our past. These six Steps turn us into an open vessel. They clear away the crud we've been carrying around and make space for self-love and self-respect. They create the new person we're becoming.

The old you, with your quirks and personality, will still be there. God needs individual personalities to create an interesting world. This includes how you dress, your sense of humor—everything that makes you uniquely you. The word *personality* isn't used here the way it is in the tradition that teaches about *Principles before personalities.* That tradition means you don't let your dislikes or fondness for certain people interfere with your spiritual growth.

Working the Steps won't turn you into a robot, an empty shell, or a clone.

Making a list of people you harmed may trigger some justification and rationalization. *I deserved to do that to him or her; that person asked for it. That person treated me worse than I treated her or him. That person hurt me first.* This Step requires letting go of anything that stands in the way of your willingness to make amends to every person you harmed.

Are you willing to clean up your side of the street, regardless of what the other person did? It's time now to clear away anything that blocks you from taking the high road no matter what other people did, or if they did it first or worse.

Activity

1. Before going to work on your list, ask yourself if you're willing to make amends to every person you've harmed. Continue asking yourself that question until you can answer yes. Even saying that you're willing to become willing is good enough.

2. If you have remnants of anger, hurt, justification, rationalization, or victimization, ask your Higher Power for help. Pray that you may be shown any incidents where your unwillingness blocks your ability to work the Eighth and Ninth Steps. Ask God to help

Activity (cont.)

you become entirely ready to let go of all that stands in the way of being totally willing. Pray that you might be shown any specific names where your attitude isn't right. Also, pray to God to remove any emotions that prevent you from correctly working this Step. Sometimes the block may be that you've become overtired. Perhaps you have been working on the past too hard. You need a break. If that's the case, take a night off. Go to a movie. Do something fun. Or just get a good night's sleep. When you feel at peace about making your list, and willingness has returned, it's time to begin. Be aware while you're working on your list that your attitude stays peaceful. If you find your body becoming tense, or should anger or defensiveness return, it's time to stop and work on your attitude again. How you feel when you're doing this is as important as what you're doing. This action is to be done with love and respect for other people and yourself. If you become frightened, remind yourself that what you're doing is very brave.

Create an Amends Directory

Gather the materials from the work you did on Steps Four and Five, buy a notebook that you'll dedicate to amends, and begin making your list. Ask God to bring to mind any names you need to remember. When you take responsibility for your behavior at this deep, profound level, all the forces in the universe gather to support you. You're not in this alone. Pay attention to the names that pop into your mind and the people you run into. Keep your notebook close by throughout the period of time you're working on your list so you can write names down immediately, before you forget them.

Five of the six "cleaning the slate" Steps refer to our harmful behaviors, each in a slightly different way. But the place they take us to, the ultimate destination, is the people we've harmed.

Step Four: Moral inventory

Step Five: Exact nature of our wrongs

Step Six: Defects of character

Step Seven: Shortcomings

Step Eight: Persons we had harmed

We started by taking an inventory of our morals. Morals include basic rights and wrongs. This would include stealing, lying, cheating, manipulating, seeking revenge, being mean or cruel, and other similar actions. We followed this by telling God, ourselves, and someone else exactly what we had done wrong. If we didn't get detailed in our Fifth Step, we'll need to do that now. Whom have we lied to, cheated on, stolen from? Whom did we betray? Have we done something to get even with someone who hurt us? Before, we were looking for behaviors. Now, we're looking for names.

In Steps Six and Seven, we looked at defects of character and shortcomings, turning them over to God and asking Him to take them. Now, we're looking for the people, businesses, and other organizations that a lack of morals, a shortcoming, or a defect caused us to directly or indirectly harm. Did we neglect our responsibilities to someone? Maybe we behaved so codependently that we loaned our rent money to someone and then we had to borrow money from someone else to pay our rent. Then we avoided that person when it came time to pay him or her back. Maybe we gave up and stopped paying our bills because we became so depressed. Did we accept paychecks from an employer but go to work and obsess all day and not do our job? That's stealing.

Sometimes we hurt the people we love most, and that's more than words to a song. We may have become so obsessed with our husband that we neglected our children or were cranky with them when they didn't deserve it. You'll need your list of behaviors, emotions, and beliefs to help you identify names too—whether or not you used that list to work the Steps.

You can start from the present and work backward. Or start at the beginning of your life and work up to now. Thoughtfully write the name of each person you've harmed. Don't let the codependent guilts get in the way. You may feel responsible for every bad thing that's ever happened in the world, but that's codependency. It's not something you actually did.

Don't worry if you can't remember the person's last name or if you don't know where someone lives. It may take weeks or months to complete the list of people you hurt depending on your age, how long you behaved codependently, and how codependent you were. Take as much time as you need to do a thorough job.

By now, your hard work has begun paying off. You're clearer and more con-nected to God, yourself, and your intuition. You're growing in self-trust, and you're also more trusting of the guidance you receive. If you sincerely ask God for help, every name that needs to be on your list will get there when it's time.

Activity

1. Be sure to keep your amends notebook close by, even at night. You may have dreams that bring back memories of someone you've hurt. It's important to enter these names right away be-fore you forget.

2. Add enough details with the name so that if you're led to make amends, you'll know what you're apologizing for. Being specific about our amends when we make them lets the person know we're sincere.

Four Kinds of Amends

There are four different ways we can make amends:

1. A face-to-face apology acknowledging what we did wrong.

2. Living amends where we add a change in behavior to a face-to-face apology. We either stop doing what hurt the person or start doing something differently so we're not neglecting the person. If we continue to hurt someone, a verbal apology won't mean much.

3. Sometimes the person we harmed is dead or we have no idea how to find him or her. Some people may have married and changed their last name. We either don't know it or forgot it. Some people may have moved and we don't know how to find them. In these and all situations, pray for guidance. We may be led to write a letter to someone who's deceased or construct a memorial in that person's memory. Each situation is unique.

4. Another kind of amends involves situations where showing up and apologizing would do more harm than good. The person may be married now, and our presence may upset his or her spouse. Maybe there's someone we've been resenting. If the person didn't know it, telling him or her would cause unnecessary hurt. In this case we could say a prayer, and in it include an apology. We also stop resenting. Maybe we had an affair, but no one knew we cheated. Bringing up the situation could do more harm than we've already done. Instead of making yourself feel better at someone else's expense, learn to either let go of or live with the guilt. We want to get rid of guilt, but we don't do it at the expense of somebody else's feelings or quality of life. Anytime there's a chance that amends could cause more harm and hurt feelings for others, pray until you're absolutely clear on the behavior that's God's will for you. Talk to someone you trust. Use good sense. You also may not want to tell everyone in your group details of your Fifth Step. Talk to God. Become willing. But take no action at all if someone could be harmed, unless and until you're certain that the amends you're planning to make is what you're meant to do.

Financial amends are a different situation. We may want a separate list for all the people we owe money to, if that's been a big problem. If we owe someone money, we come up with a clear plan—one we can stick to—and then we begin paying the person or business what we owe and apologize for being overdue. Few people bottom out without owing people money. It may not seem fair that you have to pay debts that an ex-spouse incurred, but you chose to marry that person, and unless you live in a state where legislation protects you, you're responsible for bills in the marriage, whether it was you who incurred them or your spouse. Cleaning up the damage will make the bill collectors stop calling and will build good credit. Paying bills means taking financial responsibility for ourselves, an important aspect of self-care.

Activity

1. Make and review your list of amends. To the best of your ability, indicate what kind of amends is appropriate to make to each person or organization on the list. It doesn't matter at this point if you'll actually make amends or not. Indicate if a direct apology is enough or if you need to make a living amends too, and if so, what kind. How? Put question marks by any amends where you're uncertain if making direct amends would hurt someone else or if you're confused or uncertain about what to do.

2. Make a separate list of your creditors. Contact each one. Set up a plan. Diligently make payments until all bills are paid. Many people get stuck in black-and-white thinking. *If I can't pay it all,*

Activity (cont.)

Activity (cont.)

I'll pay nothing. Then nothing gets paid. Begin making payments immediately and regularly. Stick to the plan you made. If the creditor refuses to accept anything except the entire amount or you owe money for taxes, you may need to seek help. Debtors Anonymous is a Twelve Step program for people who perpetually get into debt. Attending meetings there may be an appropriate step to take before you begin your amends. Be careful about agencies that offer help to people in debt. Some are legitimate. Others aren't. Pray for guidance about all amends on your list. Make no amends until and unless you're clear.

Direct Mending

The Eighth Step doesn't say that we make a list of all persons we've harmed, then walk around feeling guilty about it. We make a list and then, as we review it, we become willing to make amends to everyone whose name is on it. Then as we're guided, we begin the process of making direct amends.

The word *amends* is close to the word *mend*. That's what Step Nine does: It mends. We may not be able to mend our relationship with a person, but our actions mend our relationship with ourselves and our Higher Power.

"Making amends terrified me at first," said one woman, recovering from codependency. "Then, when I began to see how good I felt each time I made one, I began to enjoy the process. Each one gave me a direct jolt of self-esteem.

Sometimes if I experienced a bad day or week, I'd pull out my Eighth Step list and make amends. I knew doing that would help me feel good."

If you pray for guidance about how to make amends, you'll eventually get it. If a name of a person or organization pops into your mind while you're making your list or if you run into someone you've forgotten, put the name on your list. If the opportunity is there to make spontaneous amends and it feels right, do it. You may run into someone in your daily life, and whenever you see him or her you feel so guilty you want to run away. That may be a sign that you owe him or her amends. Put the name on the list, even if you're uncertain what you've done wrong. Then pray about it. Answers come to sincere seekers.

There's no way of knowing how people will respond to our amends. Some may refuse to see or talk to us. Others may be so angry that all they can do is yell. Most people will respond respectfully and with forgiveness. If some don't, that's not your problem. We're powerless over what other people do. We're cleaning up our past to gain a sense of self-respect and esteem. By doing this Step, we become free to go anywhere without worrying about who we'll encounter. We earn the right to walk around with our head held high and our heart open.

If the person is so angry with us that he or she becomes abusive, we don't have to let ourselves be treated badly. This program is based on forgiveness, not punishment and penance. If people use what you've done wrong to manipulate you or keep you feeling guilty, that is a game that you can't win. Don't play. However, if we owe someone money and that person is angry with us, it's still our responsibility to pay that person what we owe him or her, but we do not expose ourselves to abuse. Don't let guilt keep you in a situation where you're being punished or abused.

Remember that the Step calls for direct amends. We only write a letter or call the person on the telephone when it's impossible to meet face to face, in person. If that isn't possible, because the person is in prison or dead, then you can do the next best direct amends action.

Be as concise as possible. Stick to the point. Acknowledge what you did wrong and sincerely apologize for doing it. For living amends, or if you've relapsed several times and this isn't the first time you've made amends to this person, the less said the better. Let the person see what you're doing to change your behavior instead of talking about what you intend to do differently. In some cases, though, it may be appropriate to let the person know what he or she can reasonably expect.

We don't grovel, nor do we repeatedly beg for forgiveness if someone refuses to let us off the hook. Also, don't engage in arguing. By doing so, you're defeating the purpose of making amends. Thank the person for listening to you, leave, and then follow through with changed behaviors.

Promises, Promises

Somewhere along the line, something bigger than us kicks in. This is what it says in *Alcoholics Anonymous,* or the Big Book, on pages 83 and 84:

> **If we are painstaking about this phase of our development, we will be amazed before we are half way through.**
>
> **We are going to know a new freedom and a new happiness.**
>
> **We will not regret the past nor wish to shut the door on it.**
>
> **We will comprehend the word serenity and we will know peace.**
>
> **No matter how far down the scale we have gone, we will see how our experience can benefit others.**
>
> **That feeling of uselessness and self-pity will disappear.**
>
> **We will lose interest in selfish things and gain interest in our fellows.**
>
> **Self-seeking will slip away.**
>
> **Our whole attitude and outlook upon life will change.**
>
> **Fear of people and of economic insecurity will leave us.**
>
> **We will intuitively know how to handle situations which used to baffle us.**
>
> **We will suddenly realize that God is doing for us what we could not do for ourselves.**

———•·•———

On page v of the first edition of the *Co-Dependents Anonymous* book, it flatly states that you can expect a miraculous change in your life by working the program of Co-Dependents Anonymous.

As I make an honest effort to work the Twelve Steps and follow the Twelve Traditions . . .

1. I know a new sense of belonging. The feeling of emptiness and loneliness will disappear.

2. I am no longer controlled by my fears. I overcome my fears and act with courage, integrity and dignity.

3. I know a new freedom.

4. I release myself from worry, guilt and regret about my past and present. I am aware enough not to repeat it.

5. I know a new love and acceptance of myself and others. I feel genuinely lovable, loving and loved.

6. I learn to see myself as equal to others. My new and renewed relationships are all with equal partners.

7. I am capable of developing and maintaining healthy and loving relationships. The need to control and manipulate others will disappear as I learn to trust those who are trustworthy.

8. I learn that it is possible to mend—to become more loving, intimate and supportive. I have the choice of communicating with my family in a way which is safe for me and respectful of them.

9. I acknowledge that I am a unique and precious creation.

10. I no longer need to rely solely on others to provide my sense of worth.

11. I trust the guidance I receive from my Higher Power and come to believe in my own capabilities.

12. I gradually experience serenity, strength and spiritual growth in my daily life.

These two sets of changes that we can expect to see in ourselves are referred to as *Promises*. Maybe that's why people who are alcoholic and codependent are called Double Winners. They don't get only one set of promises. Double Winners get two sets of promises.

"When I was in treatment for chemical dependency, the people in my group used to say—only partially kidding—that *Recovery isn't any big deal. It just means changing everything about yourself and your life.* I learned that's mostly true," said one Double Winner, a member of Al-Anon and Alcoholics Anonymous. "I let go of my old relationships and behaviors. My entire life changed. But it wasn't the grueling kind of change I thought it would be. I turned into someone I never thought I could be. The Promises really do come true."

The Promises are more than words on a page, a carrot on a stick to keep us going to meetings. People may have lied to us in the past, but these Promises will manifest in the lives of people who do the work. If you work the Steps diligently, the best you can, one day you'll look around and see that they're becoming real for you. That's when *working a program, doing our work,* and *working the Steps* gets good.

I've seen more miracles as a result of people working these Steps than I've seen anywhere else. Treatment is good. Going to Twelve Step meetings and enjoying the fellowship is helpful too. But I've seen people go to groups and only talk about their problems. If you're looking for long-term change, the kind that comes from the inside out, work the Steps. They're the heart of this program, and they're the work we do. Then when you go to meetings, you can talk about the solutions too.

Activity

1. Make the amends on your list as you're guided to do. You may want to make notes on your list about what happened. This list is private. It's meant for nobody's eyes but your own. If you're doing the amends for the right reason, you'll come away from making almost every amends with your head held higher and feeling better inside. It's a natural high. If some don't go so well, shrug them off, as long as you were sincere and honestly did your part.

2. Don't forget to put your name on the list of people whom you've harmed.

Is Your Tool Kit Getting Full?

You don't need to add these two Steps to your tool kit unless you want to, because the next Step is a shortened version of this. It doesn't matter whether you work these two Steps for the mistakes you make on a daily basis or whether you work Step Ten. The idea is that you don't want to accumulate another huge glob of guilt.

Activity

1. Write about how it feels when you drop false pride and make amends for what you did wrong.

2. You can make all the amends on your list, but if you don't forgive yourself, you won't be free from guilt. If you've done your work and ongoing guilt presents a problem, look in the mirror and look into your eyes and say, "I love you and I forgive you. God forgives you too." Do this three times a day until your guilt disappears.

What If Someone Owes Me Amends?

Sometimes we've genuinely been hurt by someone's behavior, and we truly don't owe the person amends. That person may have stolen from us, lied to us, or did something else that caused deep pain. The closer we are to this person and the more we love him or her, the more the behavior can hurt. But there's only one person's program you can work: yours.

Go too deeply into trying to get someone to make amends to you, and you're getting close to crossing into the codependent zone again. If someone owes you amends and doesn't make them, it's that person's loss, not yours. If you've done your work, and worked hard at your program, you've made a large investment in recovery. That's how we make recovery our own.

Being of service, sharing your story, and going to meetings are similar to putting money in the bank. When you need to make a withdrawal from your codependency recovery account because you're thinking about getting involved with someone who isn't good for you, will you be able to go to your account, make a withdrawal, and get what you need to take care of yourself? Is your account empty or full? It's different from denial. When you see a situation that you know is bad for you, will you make a conscious choice to avoid it? Or are you going to learn another approach?

Activity

1. Keep a list of your wise choices and actions that make your recovery yours.

2. Keep another list of things that help you feel good about yourself when you're down. It might include going to a meeting, reading recovery literature, working a Step, getting involved in sponsorship (either having one or being one or both). Then the next time you feel the codependent crazies, before you call someone and moan and complain (unless that person is your sponsor), do at least two items on your list before you call. If you call your sponsor, that's probably what your sponsor will suggest you do. You may feel so balanced and centered that you don't feel the codependent crazies now. That's when it shows that you're learning how to take good care of yourself.

LESSON EIGHT:

Keep It Clean

"Much of recovery is finding

and maintaining balance in all areas

of our lives . . . as we measure our

responsibilities to ourselves and to others."

—Codependent No More

Suggested reading: chapter 20, "Learning to Live and Love Again"

STEP TEN: Continued to take personal inventory and when we were wrong, promptly admitted it.

—from the TWELVE STEPS OF CO-DEPENDENTS ANONYMOUS

The longer you're working a program, and the more you're aware of yourself and your interactions with other people, the more you'll see that someone taking responsibility for his or her own behavior is a rare and precious thing. It's far more common to see people passing the proverbial buck. "No, not me," someone says, looking right in your eyes and lying. "I didn't do that."

We may be afraid of losing our job or losing self-esteem if we admit we made a mistake. But usually, most people have a fairly good idea of who did what and when. When we don't own up, the person we're kidding the most is ourselves. We don't want to embarrass ourselves by admitting we made a mistake, but not taking responsibility for what we did—lying about it—is truly an embarrassment. To the person we're lying to, it's a slap in the face.

Why Does Something That Feels So Good Seem So Difficult to Do?

The ancient saying *The truth shall set you free* remains profoundly true.

You've gone to all the work of looking at your past and making amends. It's easier to spend some time each day or every few days taking an inventory and cleaning up your mistakes than it is to accumulate another big mess that will take months to clean up. Why not pick up after yourself as you go along?

The same caution applies here when it comes to admitting mistakes that applied in Step Five. When you contemplate admitting to something you did wrong, remember to use the qualification *except when to do so would injure them or others.* We can't buy peace of mind if someone else pays the price.

When is the best time for you to take inventory? At night, before you fall asleep? In the morning, when you first wake up and before your defense mechanism sets in? Or would you prefer to continually monitor your behaviors throughout the day? How you continue taking inventory isn't as important as getting the job done.

Then, suck it up. Yes, you may feel embarrassed for a moment, especially if you lost your cool. Our Higher Power wouldn't have given us this Step if, in His wisdom, He didn't know we'd need it. We're going to make mistakes from time to time. Some mistakes will be big ones—huge. Some mistakes will be little. No matter the size of our errors, whenever we make mistakes, we have two choices: We can close our heart and mind and detach from our conscience—piling up the guilt—or we can go to the person or people involved, and tell them the words so rarely heard on planet Earth: "I'm sorry. I was wrong. Will you forgive me?"

Be one of the rare people who takes personal responsibility for mistakes. Remember, guilt kills.

Activity

Did you tell a lie today, take something that wasn't yours, gossip about someone, forget to do or neglect doing something that was your responsibility? Did you have an accident, break something? Maybe you fender-dented a car. Nobody saw. You could get away with it, or could you? You'll know what you did. Did the cashier at the grocery store give you too much change? No, that wasn't God's way

Activity (cont.)

of saying, "Here's a little extra money." The cashier will need to make up for it at the end of the shift. Maybe you got caught up in something—having an affair or doing something that goes against your morals. The mistake may call for a direct admission of guilt, an apology with living amends, a note to someone who's passed or who you can't locate. Maybe you did something that would hurt someone horribly if you admitted to it. Don't take the easy way out, getting it off your chest so you can feel better at the other person's expense. Stop doing it. Ask God to forgive you. Then forgive yourself.

Be a man among men, a woman among women. If you're wrong, say so. Promptly admit it.

There's no other quick, daily way to use this Step. This Step was written for daily use. You're growing and changing. Get in the habit of stopping that obsessive focus on others and become more aware of yourself.

Whenever you're ready, feel free to move to Lesson Nine. Your hard work is over. Really. I promise. The Steps you're at now are rewarding and fun. Said one recovering codependent and addict, "The reason I didn't have a slip—even when I became tempted—is that I remembered how much hard work it took to work these Steps the long way," she said. "I didn't want to have to do it again."

Finding and Aligning with Your Purpose

"Get quiet. Detach. Pray. Meditate.

Ask Him what He wants us to do.

Ask to be given the power to do that.

Then let go and watch what happens."

———————————————————————————

—Codependent No More

Suggested reading: review Step Eleven in chapter 18, "Work a Twelve Step Program"

STEP ELEVEN: Sought through prayer and meditation to improve our conscious contact with God as we understood God, praying only for knowledge of God's will for us and the power to carry that out.

—from the TWELVE STEPS OF CO-DEPENDENTS ANONYMOUS

S tep Eleven gives us many gifts. It's uplifting. It tells us the kingdom of heaven is near.

I love this Step. Maybe it's because it doesn't involve the grueling drudgery of clearing out the junk from the past. Instead of looking back, we're creating today and tomorrow. Instead of preparing ourselves to find our purpose, we're living God's plan for us now. This Step also comes with a guarantee, at least that's my interpretation. We never have to do more than we can, and we'll be given all the power we need to accomplish what we're meant to do in God's timing.

Prayer and Meditation

Undeniably, prayer changes things. One short prayer asking for help can make it possible to do something we've been trying unsuccessfully to do for minutes or years. We need to remember two important conditions: There's a difference between thinking about praying and meditating, and actually doing those behaviors. Contemplating meditating is different from contemplative meditation. The second condition I've found, while seeking to make conscious contact with a Higher Power, is that prayers need to be humble and sincere. Saying please and thank you helps too.

Writer Earnie Larsen helped popularize this definition of insanity: doing the same thing over and over while expecting different results. I would like to add my own thoughts here. I think it is insane to put off prayer and meditation, because the results of doing Step Eleven can be so profound. Yet many of us avoid this Step. You can work this Step wherever you are and whenever you please, and it costs nothing. A way to connect with true power and good feelings doesn't get much better or easier than that. This Step is how you become one with God's will for you. It's how you align your will with His Divine Plan and purpose for your life. Doesn't it make you want to just pray and meditate right now?

We never know where God's will might lead us. There are no limits to divine purpose. There are places to go, things to see, emotions to feel, and people to meet beyond our wildest comprehension or ability to imagine. Our future will be so different from our past that there's no way we can visualize it. How can we when we've not experienced anything even close to it before?

We can get anywhere in the world from wherever we are. The vehicle that transports us from Point A—where we are now—to Point B—where we're going—isn't a plane, train, automobile, bus, or bicycle. It's working the Eleventh Step.

Activity

1. Do you pray and meditate? Why or why not? How often? How many years, months, or weeks have you been doing these two practices?

2. Would you like more power and more good feelings? Would you like the assurance that you're fulfilling God's purpose? If the answer is yes, all you need to do is work this Step.

The Practices

Most people agree that praying is how we talk to God, and meditating is how we listen to Him. This Step is about communicating with our Higher Power, establishing conscious contact instead of occasionally and accidentally running into Him. It's about doing these behaviors with discipline. Many people have heard the saying *One day at a time,* but they live their entire lives waiting for tomorrow to come. They are not present for the moment they're in. Present-moment living doesn't hold us back. It's how we soar. We stop focusing on outcomes. We don't ask the person we're dating where the relationship is going. We don't fantasize about all the money, fame, and fortune we'll achieve from the work we're doing.

We're with the people we're with because we want to be with them. We're doing the work for the sake of the work. Being present for someone with no expectations and wanting is what true love is, according to author Eckhart Tolle in *A New Earth: Awakening to Your Life's Purpose.*

How do we learn to be present and aware? By practicing prayer and meditation. Years ago in aikido class (aikido is a soft martial art), a famous sensei visited the class. After teaching for two hours, she opened the class to questions. We wanted to know what techniques we could practice that would most increase our power.

"That's simple," she said. "Practice meditation. Praying helps too."

Although this Step says to pray only for knowledge of God's will for us and the power to carry that out, I don't think it's wrong to mention special requests. We're building a personal relationship with our Higher Power. Why should there be limits on what we can say to Him or talk to Him about?

Asking God to bless people can be extremely important for them and us. It's the only way I've ever known that truly relieves us of resentments. We don't have to mean it when we pray. We can *Act as if.* But if we ask God to bless a person we resent each time that person's name crosses our minds and we become riled, one day we'll find ourselves asking God to bless that person and we'll actually mean it.

No doubt, prayer changes things. It changes us. We can struggle to accomplish something with no success for hours, months, or years. Then we can ask God humbly and sincerely to help. In minutes we'll accomplish what we couldn't do by ourselves.

Praying connects us to the only true source of power in the world.

I believe it's okay to ask for special requests for ourselves and others as long as we ask and don't demand or expect. What we're promised in this Step is that we'll receive knowledge of God's will for us and the power to carry it out. When you think about it, other than using our powers to help cocreate our life, what more could we want?

"I applied for a job. I'm so worried I won't get it," a woman new to codependency recovery said to me one day. "Would you please ask God to make sure I get it?" she asked next.

"What's to worry about?" I asked her. "If it's not God's will, would you even want it?"

She thought about my question a while. "Yes," she said.

I wouldn't. If it's not God's will, getting it or having it won't accomplish any purpose. It probably won't feel good, and likely it won't work. We'll be given the power to carry out God's will for us, not self-will. Besides, who better knows exactly what we need than our Higher Power, the God who created us?

When people say, "Be careful what you ask for because you might get it," what they're really saying is, "Align your will with God's purpose and plan so that when things happen, you can trust that it's God's purpose and plan for you. Pray. Tell God what's in your heart and on your mind. Ask for whatever you want, but take care to say, 'Thy will be done.'"

You may want to use prewritten prayers from your religion. Maybe you want to write your prayers yourself. Or you can just talk to God, the way you'd talk to a friend. The choice is yours. The goal we're seeking is *improving our conscious contact with God.* That means we want to climb higher and higher and become more aware of and focused on God's presence, what we say to Him, and what God says to us.

Most people grow and change in their practices of the disciplines of prayer and meditation over time. Many people fear, when it comes to meditation, that how they're doing it isn't good enough. Some people use books written by someone else that focus on an uplifting thought for each day. Other people use Eastern techniques, sitting cross-legged on the floor, eyes closed, mind stilled, either focusing on one pure thought or emptying the mind and letting God fill it with whatever He wants them to hear.

You can't pray or meditate incorrectly. You may feel awkward at first. You may procrastinate, thinking *I'm too busy, I don't have time.* That's like saying you're too busy to put gas in your car. You're late and you need to get where you're going. But then you become really delayed because you run out of gas and have to call a towing service.

Praying and meditating is how we get our power.

"When I graduated from treatment for chemical dependency, my counselor told me to be sure to remember to do four things every day," said one recovering Double Winner. "That's been thirty years ago. I can only remember two: Ask God every morning for knowledge of His will for me and the power to carry it out. Then thank Him every night for doing that and helping me get through the day. Those two things must be enough," he said. "Praying twice a day has kept me straight all these years, and despite my resistance, it got me into Al-Anon—a place I thought I'd never be found. Practicing this Step got me sober, got me into Al-Anon, and made me grateful that I'm a Double Winner. This Step can take anyone anywhere they want to go."

Activity

1. Are you running on empty or running late? Have you taken the time to pray and meditate? Did you ask God to help you, to show you His will? If you did, what happened? If you didn't, why not?

2. Are you prepared to make a commitment to grow in your conscious contact with your Higher Power? Set a goal, but keep it reasonable. How often would you like to pray? Meditate? Remember that practicing these two behaviors can make all the difference in the world.

Understanding God's Will

A question that's been around Twelve Step programs for a long time is "How do I know if something is God's will for me or not?"

When I first began recovering from codependency and started learning about owning my power, I thought power meant beating my chest and saying, "I am woman, hear me roar." It felt like there was little that I couldn't do, now that I found and owned my power. Then someone handed me a copy of the book *The Tao of Pooh*, written by Benjamin Hoff. I read it and at first became terribly confused.

I'd been learning about ideas such as owning my power. Now this book talked about Winnie-the-Poohing our way through life. No beating on the chest. We don't generate events by using power. We let go. We surrender to each experience, like Winnie-the-Pooh and his friends, whether that means falling into a hole and trying to get out, running out of honey, or trying to get the lid off the jar.

This way of living felt diametrically opposed to what I thought I was supposed to do. Maybe I needed to beat my fists on my chest and roar for a while to get up off the floor and stop being a doormat. But now, life began teaching me another way.

I began to see that we don't own power. It's something we're all connected to, the way we're connected to God, the universe, and each other. When we get out of the way, the power of the universe gets channeled through us. We opened this connection by cleaning up the past. Then we connect with power by practicing the disciplines of prayer and meditation recommended in this Step.

We pray for knowledge of God's will for us and the power to carry it out. We meditate and listen to what God wants to say. We show up for life each day, whether we want to or not. We surrender to whatever experience we find ourselves in. At first we may think that the situation we find ourselves in is an accident or mistake. We'll try to make the problem or experience go away. Then the lights turn on. We get it. We're in the midst of learning another lesson. What we're supposed to do is let go.

By living through each experience and allowing God and life to work things out in us, by relaxing into our life the way we'd sit back in a big, comfortable easy chair, we'll be guided about what to do next.

This new way of living was a huge shift, 180 degrees, from what I thought it would be when I first began recovering. But it's the best way of living I've experienced. Everything happens for a reason. If we make a mistake, no matter what it is, it can be used for good. We don't have to make life happen. Life and love happen naturally through us.

How do we know if a particular action is God's will for us? I can't give you a set of rules. But I can share some of what I've learned. Pray and meditate about decisions, although some windows of opportunity are brief and we need to decide quickly. If we get a good intuitive feeling about something, it's probably because the answer is *Yes, this is God's will.* But we won't know for certain. There are no guarantees. If we get a bad feeling, it likely means that it isn't God's will. If we get a neutral feeling, it's usually because it doesn't matter that much whether we do that thing or not. It won't affect our lives that much one way or another.

More than anything, I've learned that if we're working the Steps and praying and meditating—even a little—God's will for us is whatever we find ourselves doing right now.

Are you familiar with navigation systems for automobiles? If you make a wrong turn, the navigation system recalculates and tells you how to get to your destination. No matter how many mistakes you make, it will continue to recalculate and direct your route. God's will is similar to a navigation system. No matter how many wrong turns we make, we can get home from wherever we are.

Activity

1. How do you decide what God's will is for you? Do you tend to think things through, feel your way through life, or do some of each? Do you use intuition? Keep track of the decisions you make, how you make them, and how they work out.

Activity (cont.)

149

Activity (cont.)

❷ Is someone trying to control your will by telling you what to do? If so, who? Are you allowing it or setting boundaries? Sometimes it can be seductive to let someone control us, at least for a while. In the end, it doesn't work out well. Are you trying to play God with someone else? Who? What's the reason for what you're doing?

❸ Find a system that helps you discern God's will for you. Remember that rarely, if ever, do we have to make a decision until and unless we're clear.

Discovering Your True Powers

One symptom that marks a codependent is an unrealistic relationship with power. Codependents sometimes waste years of their lives trying to do things they can't. They attempt to exert powers that they don't have and never will, such as controlling others. It's not our right or responsibility to interfere with another person's free will. In the process of trying to do what we can't, we overreach our true powers. We also become too exhausted from controlling and obsessing to do much else except pass out every night from the stress of obsession.

Some people who are not in a recovery program object to the Twelve Steps. Some of these people claim they don't need to admit powerlessness, and that doing so unnecessarily holds people back. I don't believe that's true. When we admit powerlessness over things we truly can't do, all we're doing is telling the truth.

Some people don't take recovery far enough. They discover what they're powerless over, but they don't discover their powers. They don't find out what they're capable of doing. Or they limit their lives by a preconceived notion of what God's will is. For instance, if people believe that suffering is necessary, that sacrificing all desires is required, that's going to inhibit their beliefs and understanding of what God's will is for their life.

"Shortly after my divorce I found myself in a dilemma," said Annie E., who identifies herself as a recovering codependent. "I was walking down the street one day feeling distraught. I'd spent years building my own business. Although I wasn't at the pinnacle of success, I'd come a long way, but not far enough to have benefits like insurance for myself and the children. I loved my business. It meant so much to me. I felt awful because I believed now I would have to give it up, take a nine-to-five job, and get all the security that would bring. That meant a huge loss. I'd worked so hard. But I had to do what I had to do to take care of my children," she said.

"Then an idea occurred to me so clearly it was like someone was putting thoughts in my head. 'What makes you think that you have to do anything other than pray for God's will for you and the power to carry it out every day now that you're divorced?' *That's a good point,* I thought. *Why did I think God's will meant I couldn't do what I loved doing—as long as I asked Him every day to show me His will and give me the power to carry it out?* I realized it was because I believed I was supposed to suffer. In the end, I didn't give up my business. Eventually I got insurance and gave myself benefits. I made enough to raise my children, send them to college, and take care of myself. I'm still working at my business that I almost talked myself out of, thinking it couldn't possibly be God's will."

This Step doesn't limit us. It's the pathway to almost unlimited power—as long as we align ourselves with God's will through prayer and meditation.

What are some of our essential God-given powers? We can feel our own feelings, think, solve problems, let go, and learn new behaviors. We can work these Twelve Steps. We can learn to express who we are. We can ask directly for what we want and need. We can learn to set healthy boundaries, and then we can enforce them. We can learn healthy ways to give to and nurture other people and ourselves. We can learn to take care of ourselves. We can take financial responsibility for ourselves. Plus we can set and achieve our goals based on our own unique set of abilities, skills, gifts, and desires.

"I wish to God that I would have begun setting goals for myself that involved using my creativity earlier in recovery," said one woman, a recovering codependent. "I was in recovery for years before realizing I could set goals to do things I felt passionate about."

I began my writing career one day when I was pregnant with Shane, my son who died. I was painting a room to get ready before his birth. Suddenly I remembered a dream I'd had since the age of five or six. I'd always wanted to be a writer. I loved writing stories and wanted to write all my life. How could I forget something I'd felt so strongly about? I looked up at the ceiling and said a prayer, "God, I don't have the first idea about how to go about becoming a writer. I don't have a college degree. I don't have a clue if it's your will for me. So if you want me to be a writer, you're going to have to show me what to do, when to do it, and how."

Within twenty-four hours, I had a job writing stories for a community newspaper. I received five dollars for each story. I prayed throughout my career. I meditated. I specifically turned my career over to God's care. *Show me what you want me to write, and when you want me to write it* has been my writer's prayer from the beginning. I also set specific goals. But after each list of goals, I'd write *Thy will be done.*

My goal was to be a professional writer, to have a publishing contract before I wrote a manuscript, and to get paid for my work. From that day on, I had an assignment and was paid for everything I wrote.

While I believe in setting goals and encourage people to follow the dreams of their heart, it's also important to ask ourselves why we want what we do. Is it to grab on to the big brass ring, or is it part of our path of service? I didn't want to be a writer to be famous. I wanted to write so I could be the eyes and ears for the people in the community where I lived. I wanted to be of service by communicating to them in a way they could grasp and understand, because that's how I liked ideas communicated to me.

I also worked more of the Twelve Steps on my career. More about that in the next and final lesson.

Activity

1 Have you begun discovering and using your true powers as well as admitting your powerlessness? Have you turned the use of these powers, abilities, and gifts over to the care of your Higher Power?

2 List your powers, abilities, gifts, skills, and talents. Also list how you use and express them. If you have trouble getting started, begin with any gifts or strengths people have told you that you have. Ask people who know you well what they see as your gifts, strengths, and skills. Then ask your Higher Power to reveal your strengths, powers, skills, assets, talents, and gifts to you in a way you can believe and understand.

3 Sometimes our weaknesses and character defects can be turned over, and the flip side of them is a strength. We may be care-takers, but the strength is we're good at helping others feel good about themselves.

4 Go back to your childhood. Is there something you wanted to be when you were young? Were you good at something in school? What, and why did you stop doing it? Keep at this list all of your life. In the past years, I learned how to do three things that I never dreamt I'd be able to do. One was learning accounting skills

Activity (cont.)

Activity (cont.)

when the court appointed me conservator for my mother. I had to have a woman with a mathematics degree teach me how to do a financial balance sheet. It twisted my head in circles, but eventually I learned how. I ended up doing an excellent job, and the final account balanced to the penny. Now I'm learning how to build Web sites. I also got my license to skydive. I learned how to jump out of planes. Stay open and be willing to learn to do something new. Old dogs can learn new tricks, and this dog still hunts! Some of our life lessons are about spiritual growth. Sometimes our lesson is to learn to do something new and different, to stretch our mind beyond limits we've placed on ourselves. No matter what we're learning, it takes time. We need to start where we're at, and move forward from there. Don't expect to start at the top.

5 Constantly set new written goals. Keep a fresh, updated goal list as long as you're alive. This will help you create and maintain a life. Call it a wish list, goal list, whatever you want. There's so much power in the written word. Write your goals, then let go of them. Keep your list in a private, sacred place. You'll be surprised when you look back and see how many goals became realities and how many dreams came true.

Reaching the Mountaintop

"... *acts of kindness are not kind*

unless we feel good about ourselves, what we are doing,

and the person we are doing it for."

—Codependent No More

Suggested reading: "What's a Rescue?" in chapter 8, "Remove the Victim"

STEP TWELVE: Having had a spiritual awakening as the result of these steps, we tried to carry this message to other co-dependents, and to practice these principles in all our affairs.

—from the TWELVE STEPS OF CO-DEPENDENTS ANONYMOUS

I shouldn't need to hold your hand anymore to help you reach the top of the mountain. You're almost there. You've done so much work. You've learned so much. Read through the Step at the beginning of this lesson. Can you identify and describe the three actions that this Step suggests we do? As you read the Step, you can substitute another word for the word *codependents.* We can use *others, other parents of addicts, other spouses of alcoholics*—whatever fits and works for us. We don't have to make an issue of substituting this word if we're attending a meeting, one that's following the traditions. They'll want to stick to their wording of this Step. But that doesn't have to stop you from using the word or words you want to use quietly, in the privacy of your mind.

To disrupt the group by making an issue of how you're going to do this Step likely won't bring good results. By now, you should be able to trust yourself.

Three Actions

Let's look at the actions requested by this Step. The first action is something that should relieve you. It's passive. Well, not completely passive. It's a gift you've received from all the hard work you've done on yourself and these Steps.

I had a two-part spiritual awakening while writing this book. One was that working these Steps is an enormous amount of work. But the second part of that awakening was that when we're actually doing the work, we receive all the power and guidance we need to do it. *Simple but not easy* is another program saying that's true.

157

The first action in this Step states that we will have had a spiritual awakening as a result of working these Steps. What that means will be unique to each of us, and it will happen to us. The second action is carrying the message to others. We don't carry others by taking responsibility for them and their actions. We carry the message and let people carry themselves.

The third action is practicing the principles in these Steps in all areas of our life. That means we can apply these Steps in any area of our life that gets or feels out of control, from relationships to finances, to our job, to parenting, to remodeling our house. Anything is fair game and will respond to the application of these principles.

These principles will become our living skills for the rest of our lives if we choose to let them. That choice is up to us.

Activity

1. Keep track of your spiritual awakening or awakenings, those times when you feel God in your life so strongly you can't deny it. Write about it as much as you can so when you're feeling alone or depressed, you can read it and reassure yourself that you're not alone. You may define a spiritual experience as seeing progress or changes in yourself. The first time you respond to a fearful situation by evaluating what you can control and what you can't, doing what you can, then letting go of the rest, is definitely a spiritual experience for any of us who identify as codependents. But many other events may qualify too. That's your choice, and the result of evaluating your daily experiences.

Activity (cont.)

❷ Keep track of how you carry the message to others, including the message you carry, to whom, how you do it, what the results are, and how you feel about what you've done. We'll discuss that in greater detail later.

❸ Keep track of other areas of your life where you work these Steps and the results you experience from doing that. That means work the Steps by changing the wording in your head, on specific areas of your life as problems and challenges spin out of control or begin to cause you pain. By now you should be assured that these principles or Steps really work.

Spiritual Awakenings

"I don't know why—maybe God knew I needed it to happen this way—but I'm a Double Winner. I didn't have my spiritual awakenings as a result of working these Steps. I had them first. Each was so profound I couldn't deny the importance of moving forward and working these Steps," said one Double Winner.

The Big Book, or *Alcoholics Anonymous,* states that for some the experience of spiritual awakening may happen gradually over a period of time. For others, it may manifest in one loud, delightful spiritual explosion.

I can't predict the nature of your spiritual experience. However, you will awaken spiritually by hurling yourself into working these Steps with all the passion and enthusiasm you have used to control another person or to take care of others. Whether it's at the beginning or somewhere between working Steps One through Twelve, you will awaken spiritually.

Activity

1. Part of a spiritual awakening for someone suffering from codependency is learning that you are real. You count. You matter. You have a life. You deserve to be free of abuse. More than that, you can take care of yourself. Talk to other people who have worked the Steps on codependency issues. Ask them if they'd share with you the nature of their spiritual awakening.

2. Ask your Higher Power for a spiritual awakening designed for you. My favorite prayer is this: "God, I need to feel your hand, your touch, in a way I cannot deny that it's You." No greater feeling exists for me than to see proof that God knows my name, knows where I live, and cares about my life.

Carrying the Message

Many ways exist to carry the message, according to Twelve Step literature. We can sponsor someone. Sponsorship means we agree to have a special relationship with someone in the program and preferably a member of the same sex. We'll meet with that person outside meetings and work on issues and problems in greater detail with her or him.

Being a role model is a way to carry the message. That means living a life that stands out as one that others admire and desire for themselves. They want what we have, but it's not our money, home, or spouse they desire. It's the way we work our program and our way of life.

We can carry the message by speaking at meetings. Just attending meetings can help others. If someone is ill or in the hospital, we can visit.

We can be of service by helping set up the room where meetings are held, or cleaning up after the meeting finishes. Or we can volunteer to be secretary or treasurer of the group. Sharing our recovery story at meetings is another way we carry the message. Taking your turn and talking about the solution can be particularly helpful. Anyone can go on and on endlessly, complaining about what hurts. While that may be necessary and important for a while, it's also important in meetings—especially for people recovering from codependency—to share with the group how working a Step solved a problem.

In the first lesson I wrote this, but it bears repeating: The biggest shortcoming of the codependency recovery movement is that codependents frequently don't take working the Steps as seriously as alcoholics and addicts. They think it's an option, often because they haven't been the ones using drugs or drinking. While these Steps are suggested, not mandatory, they're the vehicle by which we change and grow. If we don't work them, not much is going to happen. The Promises and spiritual awakenings are for those who work these Steps. I've often seen what happens to people who go to meetings but don't work the Steps. They remain perpetual victims, mostly of themselves and their own behaviors and actions. The Twelve Steps are similar to climbing the mountains in China. If you don't climb the steps, you don't get to the temple at the top. You can stand and watch others climb and reach the temple. But you won't move up unless you climb the steps yourself.

"I've seen and had the message carried to me in many ways," said one woman in Al-Anon. "At the first meeting I attended, I saw other people—and that included some living in and with situations much worse than mine—who were happy, serene, and peaceful. They weren't being controlled by someone else's behavior. They were the captain of their own ships. They made it clear that this happened by working the Twelve Steps."

Another man described the message that he received this way: "I'm a Double Winner. My son's behavior was out of control and destroying our family life. I learned that I didn't have to engage in his insanity. I didn't have to be controlled by his behavior. Most of all, it wasn't my job to control him."

"The message that someone carried to me was that I'd become as out of control as the alcoholic," said one woman, another Double Winner. "If I wanted to find peace, sanity, serenity, and a desire to live, I needed to work two programs. Even though I wasn't crazy about the idea at first, I needed to work the Steps again, this time on my codependency."

"I could think, I could feel, I could take care of myself. I could solve my problems and let go of what I couldn't solve. That's the message someone carried to me. It changed my life," another recovering codependent said.

Of all the messages I've heard, this is my favorite: "I can detach with love. I can't control anything with worry. I can trust God, even when I'm not certain I can," said A. J., a recovering codependent. "And rarely are things as I perceive them."

We'll get the message we most need when we need it. When we get out of the way and stop trying to control people and work the Eleventh Step by striving to do God's will for us, we'll be the message carrier for others. We give and we get.

Activity

What message did someone carry to you when you needed it?

What's the message you're carrying now?

Practice Won't Make Us Perfect

These principles show us how God wants us to live, and they help us live that way. Often, religious principles can be confusing, complex, and open to an extremely wide range of interpretation, from behaving codependently to killing others and starting war. That's not to say there's anything wrong with religions. They're beautiful, each one, in its pure form. Unfortunately, people often manipulate the ideas from a beautiful religion into something full of hatred and control.

The principles of the Twelve Steps work well in any area of our lives where we're having trouble. That's likely why so many different kinds of Twelve Step groups have begun. From dealing with financial problems to eating disorders, gambling, sexually acting out, having to be in love, suffering from phobias, and excessive fear and anxiety, if these Steps are applied to the problem, they'll be the solution.

The more we practice these Steps, the easier they become. But I haven't yet met anyone who works them perfectly. That's why we've been given the slogan *Progress not perfection.*

All you need to do is your best. Your Higher Power will take care of the rest. Your needs will be met. Your lessons will come to you, when it's time—one after another. You're being refined. You're becoming a new person.

Activity

Maybe we'll come face to face some day. Maybe we won't. Maybe you won't go to groups, but you can still carry the message. Someone carried a message to me when my son died, in the intensive care unit. A nurse put her hand on my shoulder. "This is going to be the hardest thing you've ever experienced. It'll take about eight years. But you'll get through it," she said. "I know because my daughter died when she was nine." I didn't want to hear anything she had to say because I didn't want to accept that my son was dead. But eight years later, I found myself walking up to a woman whose son had just died. I didn't think about it. This happened naturally. I put my hand on her shoulder. "This is going to be the hardest thing you'll ever go through. It'll take about eight years. But you'll get through it," I said. "I know because my son died when he was twelve."

Live a life of service. Carry the message. Be as calm, happy, and serene as you can. You'll get out of life what you give to it. May blessings, luck, and good fortune be with you as you fulfill your life purpose and find your destiny.

BIBLIOGRAPHY

Alcoholics Anonymous, Fourth Edition. New York: AA World Services, 2002.

Beattie, Melody. *Choices: Taking Control of Your Life and Making It Matter.* San Francisco: HarperOne, 2003.

Brandhagen, Dean. "Addictionz" Web site (www.addictionz.com), a collection of Twelve Step sayings, slogans, Steps, and traditions.

Co-Dependents Anonymous, First Edition. Denver: CoDA Resource Publishing, 1995.

Gawain, Shakti. *Creative Visualization: Use the Power of Your Imagination to Create What You Want in Your Life.* Novato, CA: Nataraj Publishing, 1978.

Hill, Napoleon. *The Law of Success: The Master Wealth-Builder's Complete and Original Lesson Plan for Achieving Your Dreams.* New York: Tarcher/Penguin, 2008.

Tolle, Eckhart. *A New Earth: Awakening to Your Life's Purpose.* New York: Plume/Penguin, 2006.

APPENDIX A:

The Twelve Steps of Various Organizations

ALCOHOLICS ANONYMOUS

1. We admitted we were powerless over alcohol—that our lives had become unmanageable.

2. Came to believe that a Power greater than ourselves could restore us to sanity.

3. Made a decision to turn our will and our lives over to the care of God *as we understood Him.*

4. Made a searching and fearless moral inventory of ourselves.

5. Admitted to God, to ourselves, and to another human being the exact nature of our wrongs.

6. Were entirely ready to have God remove all these defects of character.

7. Humbly asked Him to remove our shortcomings.

8. Made a list of all persons we had harmed, and became willing to make amends to them all.

9. Made direct amends to such people wherever possible, except when to do so would injure them or others.

10. Continued to take personal inventory and when we were wrong promptly admitted it.

11. Sought through prayer and meditation to improve our conscious contact with God, *as we understood Him,* praying only for knowledge of His will for us and the power to carry that out.

12. Having had a spiritual awakening as the result of these steps, we tried to carry this message to alcoholics, and to practice these principles in all our affairs.

CO-DEPENDENTS ANONYMOUS (CODA)

1. We admitted we were powerless over others—that our lives had become unmanageable.

2. Came to believe that a Power greater than ourselves could restore us to sanity.

3. Made a decision to turn our will and our lives over to the care of God as we understood God.

4. Made a searching and fearless moral inventory of ourselves.

5. Admitted to God, to ourselves, and to another human being the exact nature of our wrongs.

6. Were entirely ready to have God remove all these defects of character.

7. Humbly asked God to remove our shortcomings.

8. Made a list of all persons we had harmed and became willing to make amends to them all.

9. Made direct amends to such people wherever possible, except when to do so would injure them or others.

10. Continued to take personal inventory and when we were wrong, promptly admitted it.

11. Sought through prayer and meditation to improve our conscious contact with God as we understood God, praying only for knowledge of God's will for us and the power to carry that out.

12. Having had a spiritual awakening as the result of these steps, we tried to carry this message to other co-dependents, and to practice these principles in all our affairs.

AL-ANON/ALATEEN

1. We admitted we were powerless over alcohol—that our lives had become unmanageable.

2. Came to believe that a Power greater than ourselves could restore us to sanity.

3. Made a decision to turn our will and our lives over to the care of God *as we understood Him.*

4. Made a searching and fearless moral inventory of ourselves.

5. Admitted to God, to ourselves, and to another human being the exact nature of our wrongs.

6. Were entirely ready to have God remove all these defects of character.

7. Humbly asked Him to remove our shortcomings.

8. Made a list of all persons we had harmed, and became willing to make amends to them all.

9. Made direct amends to such people wherever possible, except when to do so would injure them or others.

10. Continued to take personal inventory and when we were wrong promptly admitted it.

11. Sought through prayer and meditation to improve our conscious contact with God *as we understood Him,* praying only for knowledge of His will for us and the power to carry that out.

12. Having had a spiritual awakening as the result of these steps, we tried to carry this message to others, and to practice these principles in all our affairs.

GAM-ANON

1. We admitted we were powerless over the problem in our family.

2. Came to believe that a power greater than ourselves could restore us to a normal way of thinking and living. Gam-Anon states that a belief in a Higher Power along with an honest look at themselves will help to resolve their fears, worries, and suspicions.

3. Made a decision to turn our will and our lives over to the care of this power of our own understanding. Step three is the willingness to accept the will of a Higher Power and to let go of self-will. Self-will is said to be at the very root of bitterness, worries, and unhappiness among Gam-Anon members.

4. Made a searching and fearless moral inventory of ourselves. This can be a very difficult step since most Gam-Anon members have been blaming the gambler for his or her own shortcomings. Gam-Anon provides a list of personal assets and liabilities to use as a guideline when working on step four.

5. Admitted to ourselves and to another human being the exact nature of our wrongs. In this step one seeks out a person who can be trusted to share the information from his or her fourth step inventory. As the person "unloads" his or her past, a feeling of freedom and peace of mind enables him or her to continue growing in recovery.

6. Were entirely ready to have these defects of character removed. Recognizing and owning personal character defects in steps four and five now allow members to bring about positive change. Gam-Anon states that many of their members begin working on self-pity and resentment toward their long-term goal, which is peace of mind.

7. Humbly ask God (of our understanding) to remove our shortcomings. After becoming well aware of one's shortcomings, help is now required in order to change. Having made a decision to turn one's will over to a Higher Power in step three, it is time to humbly ask Him to remove one's shortcomings.

8. Made a list of all persons we had harmed and became willing to make amends to them all. Step eight asks for a list to be made of all those harmed. Early on it can be difficult to realize how one has harmed so many people. Harsh punishment, misdirected anger and criticizing others can be common reasons for harming family, friends, or co-workers.

9. Made direct amends to such people whenever possible except when to do so would injure them or others. Making amends to those harmed is an opportunity to bring about change in the spirit of love, kindness, and general well-being. Step nine also states that one should be careful not to hurt anyone in the process of making amends.

10. Continued to take personal inventory and when we were wrong, promptly admitted it. Complacency can lead back to old feelings and behaviors. Step ten asks to reflect on oneself on a daily basis to evaluate one's own progress or shortcomings. Step ten also requires the person to admit to any wrongdoing immediately. Following this step will lead toward spiritual growth and serenity.

11. Sought through prayer and meditation to improve our conscious contact with God, as we understood Him, praying only for knowledge of His will for us, and the power to carry that out. This step will open the door to a new and more spiritual way of living. It is suggested to start each day with a prayer or thought of one's Higher Power to make each day a better day.

12. Having made an effort to practice these principles in all our affairs, we tried to carry this message to others. Having had some measure of success in working through the other steps, it is now time to carry out the main purpose of the Gam-Anon program, which is to help others who are still suffering from the gambling problem in their home.

NAR-ANON

1. We admitted we were powerless over the addict—that our lives have become unmanageable.

2. Came to believe that a Power greater than ourselves could restore us to sanity.

3. Made a decision to turn our will and our lives over to the care of God as we understood Him.

4. Made a searching and fearless moral inventory of ourselves.

5. Admitted to God, to ourselves, and to another human being the exact nature of our wrongs.

6. Were entirely ready to have God remove all these defects of character.

7. Humbly asked Him to remove our shortcomings.

8. Made a list of all persons we had harmed, and became willing to make amends to them all.

9. Made direct amends to such people whenever possible except when to do so would injure them or others.

10. Continued to take personal inventory and when we were wrong promptly admitted it.

11. Sought through prayer and meditation to improve our conscious contact with God as we understood Him, praying only for knowledge of His will for us and the power to carry that out.

12. Having had a spiritual awakening as a result of these steps, we tried to carry this message to others, and to practice these principles in all our affairs.

CODEPENDENTS OF SEX ADDICTS (COSA)

1. We admitted we were powerless over compulsive sexual behavior—that our lives had become unmanageable.

2. Came to believe that a Power greater than ourselves could restore us to sanity.

3. Made a decision to turn our will and our lives over to the care of God as we understood God.

4. Made a searching and fearless moral inventory of ourselves.

5. Admitted to God, to ourselves, and to another human being the exact nature of our wrongs.

6. Were entirely ready to have God remove all these defects of character.

7. Humbly asked God to remove our shortcomings.

8. Made a list of all persons we had harmed, and became willing to make amends to them all.

9. Made direct amends to such people wherever possible, except when to do so would injure them or others.

10. Continued to take personal inventory and when we were wrong promptly admitted it.

11. Sought through prayer and meditation to improve our conscious contact with God as we understood God, praying only for knowledge of God's will for us and the power to carry that out.

12. Having had a spiritual awakening as the result of these steps, we tried to carry this message to others, and to practice these principles in all areas of our lives.

APPENDIX B:

Resources

Co-Dependents Anonymous (CoDA) Fellowship Services Office

P.O. Box 33577
Phoenix, AZ 85067-3577
602-277-7991 *(This number provides only meeting information)*
888-444-2359 (Toll-free)
888-444-2379 (Spanish toll-free)
www.coda.org
outreach@coda.org

Al-Anon/Alateen Family Group Headquarters

1600 Corporate Landing Parkway
Virginia, Beach, VA 23454-5617
888-4AL-ANON (888-425-2666) (Toll-free)
757-563-1600 (Phone)
757-563-1655 (Fax)
www.al-anon.alateen.org
wso@al-anon.org

Gam-Anon International Service Office, Inc.

P.O. Box 157
Whitestone, NY 11357
718-352-1671 (Phone)
718-746-2571 (Fax)
www.gam-anon.org
gamanonoffice@aol.com

Nar-Anon Family Group Headquarters, Inc.

22527 Crenshaw Blvd., Suite 200B
Torrance, CA 90505
800-477-6291 (Toll-free)
310-534-8188 (Phone)
www.nar-anon.org
naranonWSO@gmail.com

International Service Organization of Codependents of Sex Addicts (or ISO of COSA)

P.O. Box 14537
Minneapolis, MN 55414
763-537-6904 (Phone)
www.cosa-recovery.org
info@cosa-recovery.org

ABOUT THE AUTHOR

MELODY BEATTIE is one of America's most beloved self-help authors and a household name in addiction and recovery circles. Her international bestselling book, *Codependent No More,* introduced the world to the term *codependency* in 1986. Millions of readers have trusted Melody's words of wisdom and guidance because she knows firsthand what they're going through. In her lifetime, she has survived abandonment, kidnapping, sexual abuse, drug and alcohol addiction, divorce, and the death of a child. "Beattie understands being overboard, which helps her throw bestselling lifelines to those still adrift," said *Time Magazine.*

Melody was born in St. Paul, Minnesota, in 1948. Her father left home when she was a toddler, and she was raised by her mother. "My mother was a classic codependent," Melody recalls. Spanning more than twenty years, her writing career has produced fifteen books published in twenty languages and hundreds of newspaper and magazine articles. She has been a frequent guest on many national television shows, including *Oprah.* She and her books continue to be featured regularly in national publications including *Time, People,* and other major periodicals around the world.

Although it almost destroyed her when her twelve-year-old son Shane died in a ski accident in 1991, eventually Melody picked up the pieces of her life again. "I wanted to die, but I kept waking up alive," she says. She began skydiving, mountain climbing, and teaching others what she'd learned about grief.

OTHER BOOKS BY MELODY BEATTIE
available from Hazelden

hazelden.org/bookstore
800-328-9000

"Beattie understands being overboard,
which helps her throw best-selling lifelines
to those still adrift."—Time

Codependent No More:
How to Stop Controlling Others and Start Caring for Yourself

Is someone else's problem your problem? If, like so many others, you've lost sight of your own life in the drama of tending to someone else's, you may be codependent—and you may find yourself in this book. The healing touchstone of millions, this modern classic by one of America's best-loved and most inspirational authors holds the key to understanding codependency and to unlocking its stultifying hold on your life.

With instructive life stories, personal reflections, exercises, and self-tests, *Codependent No More* is a simple, straightforward, readable map of the perplexing world of codependency, charting the path to freedom and a lifetime of healing, hope, and happiness. Writing for *Newsweek* in 2009, Dr. Drew Pinsky named this volume one of the four essential self-help books available today.

Softcover: Order No. 5014
E-book: Order No. EB5014
Spanish edition, softcover: Order No. 6296

Beyond Codependency:
And Getting Better All the Time

We're learning to let go, to live our lives free of the grip of someone else's problems. Now we must master the art of self-care. Melody Beattie brings us a book about what to do once the pain has stopped and we've begun to suspect that we have a life to live. *Beyond Codependency* is about what happens next. In simple, straight-forward terms, Beattie takes us into the territory beyond codependency, into the realm of self-love and emotional maturity. With personal stories, hard-won insights, and activities, she teaches us to deal with shame, grow in self-esteem, overcome deprivation, and get beyond our fatal attractions to find relationships that work. This book "goes beyond how we hurt to how we heal," wrote Veronica Ray, author of *Choosing Happiness*.

Softcover: Order No. 5064
E-book: Order No. EB5064
Spanish edition, softcover: Order No. 7091

52 Weeks of Conscious Contact

What gets in the way of serenity? For most people, the answer is life—those every-day distractions, obligations, and frustrations that cause chaos and clutter. In this week-by-week guidebook, Melody Beattie brings new hope to those who long for a more serene life. These collections of stories, meditations, and suggestions address key self-care issues: how to nurture inner peace, when to reach out to others, how to carry through on good intentions, where to make time for fun, how to cultivate a deeper prayer life. Beattie's thoughtful prose and practical advice open new doors to reflection, affirmation, and change.

Softcover: Order No. 1984
E-book: Order No. EB1984

Gratitude:
Inspirations by Melody Beattie

> *"Today, celebrate who you are."*
> *"We can show our gratitude for life in even our smallest actions."*
> *"Could it be that you're who you are and where you are for now for a reason?"*

Featuring stirring affirmations in Beattie's own words, *Gratitude* encourages and inspires readers to reconnect with what's truly important in life. Offering a respite from today's often harried habits of living, this book's colorful pages capture the essence of everyday blessings—the twists and turns, the friends we make, and the simple pleasures that create a lasting attitude of gratitude.

Softcover: Order No. 2746
E-book: Order No. EB2746

The Grief Club:
The Secret to Getting Through All Kinds of Change

In this profoundly personal, powerfully healing book, Melody Beattie helps readers through life's most difficult times. Part memoir, part self-help book, part journalism, these stories bind together the human experience of loss in its many forms—death, divorce, drug addiction, and the tumultuous yet tender process of recovery. It's a book punctuated with Beattie's trademark candor and intuitive wisdom—a book you need to read and share.

Softcover: Order No. 2606
E-book: Order No. EB2606

The Language of Letting Go:
Daily Meditations on Codependency

Melody Beattie integrates her own life experience and recovery wisdom in this meditation book written especially for those of us who struggle with codependency. Problems are made to be solved, Beattie reminds us, and the best thing we can do is take responsibility for our own pain and self-care. This book of inspirations provides us with a thought to guide us through each day, showing us that every day brings an opportunity for growth and renewal.

Softcover: Order No. 5076
E-book: Order No. EB5076
Spanish edition, softcover: Order No. 6402

More Language of Letting Go:
366 New Daily Meditations

Relationships need tending—and who better to turn to for focus and encouragement than Melody Beattie? In this, the companion to the best-selling *Language of Letting Go,* she offers 366 fresh essays, meditations, and activities to help us let go of codependent tendencies and cultivate healthy, balanced relationships. In her characteristically direct, unsentimental style, Beattie distills compassionate insights on how best to nurture our spiritual and emotional lives. These profound and beautifully articulated thoughts, one for each day of the year, cover topics from trust in the future to the art of gratitude.

Softcover: Order No. 1976
E-book: Order No. EB1976

Playing It by Heart:
Taking Care of Yourself No Matter What

Since the publication of the groundbreaking *Codependent No More,* millions of people have confronted the demons of codependency. And yet many in recovery later find themselves slipping back into the old ways that brought them such grief. In this book, Melody Beattie helps readers understand what drives them back into the grasp of controlling behavior and victimhood—and what it takes to pull themselves out, to return to the healing, faith, and maturity that come with a commitment to recovery.

Personal essays, inspiring anecdotes, and prescriptive reminders show readers how to stop acting out their painful obsessions. Drawing on the wisdom of Twelve Step healing, Christianity, and Eastern religions, Beattie explores her own most intense personal lessons and shows readers that, despite setbacks, recovery is a lifelong opportunity for spiritual growth.

Softcover: Order No. 8604
E-book: Order No. EB8604

Stop Being Mean to Yourself:
A Story About Finding the True Meaning of Self-Love

"Melody Beattie gives you the tools to discover the magnificence and splendor of your being," wrote Deepak Chopra, M.D., of this "wonderfully practical book." Beckoning readers toward new spiritual territory, Beattie conducts us through teeming Casablanca, war-torn Algeria, and the caverns of Egypt's great pyramids as she embarks on a fresh journey of the soul.

An enlightening blend of travel adventure and spiritual discovery, filled with new ideas for overcoming the pitfalls of guilt and self-doubt, *Stop Being Mean to Yourself* is a compassionate tour guide for the troubled and the heartsick, for those who seek a happier place in the world. A tale that is at once modern and timeless, rich with the promise of personal discovery, this book reveals the art of living and of loving others—and ourselves. As full of suspense and excitement as it is of hope and encouragement, it is as rewarding for its pure reading pleasure as for the wisdom it imparts.

Softcover: Order No. 1054
E-book: Order No. EB1054

HAZELDEN, a national nonprofit organization founded in 1949, helps people reclaim their lives from the disease of addiction. Built on decades of knowledge and experience, Hazelden offers a comprehensive approach to addiction that addresses the full range of patient, family, and professional needs, including treatment and continuing care for youth and adults, research, higher learning, public education and advocacy, and publishing.

A life of recovery is lived "one day at a time." Hazelden publications, both educational and inspirational, support and strengthen lifelong recovery. In 1954, Hazelden published *Twenty-Four Hours a Day,* the first daily meditation book for recovering alcoholics, and Hazelden continues to publish works to inspire and guide individuals in treatment and recovery, and their loved ones. Professionals who work to prevent and treat addiction also turn to Hazelden for evidence-based curricula, informational materials, and videos for use in schools, treatment programs, and correctional programs.

Through published works, Hazelden extends the reach of hope, encouragement, help, and support to individuals, families, and communities affected by addiction and related issues.

For questions about Hazelden publications, please call **800-328-9000** or visit us online at **hazelden.org/bookstore.**